New Religious Movements Series
Series Editor: Peter B. Clarke

BLACK PARADISE
The Rastafarian Movement

In the same series

MY SWEET LORD: THE HARE KRISHNA MOVEMENT
Kim Knott

THE WAY OF THE HEART: THE RAJNEESH MOVEMENT
Judith Thompson and Paul Heelas

BLACK PARADISE
The Rastafarian Movement

PETER B. CLARKE

The Centre for New Religious Movements,
King's College, London

R. Reginald

San Bernardino, California
MCMLXXXVII

First published 1986

© PETER B. CLARKE 1986

British Library Cataloguing in Publication Data

Clarke, Peter B. (Peter Bernard)
    Black paradise: the Rastafarian movement.
    1. Ras Tafari movement — Great Britain
    I. Title
    305.6'996   BL2532.R37

ISBN 0-85030-428-8

The Aquarian Press is part of the Thorsons Publishing Group

Printed and bound in Great Britain

Contents

Series Editor's Preface

New religions abound in contemporary Britain. As many as five hundred have been established since 1945. These religions derive from many different cultures and have given rise to much controversy in the media and in every walk of life — politics, medicine, education, the law, and the churches.

The methods of recruitment, aims, purposes, rituals, and practices of a number of these movements have all been hotly debated and observers have been led to ask to what extent, if any, some of these movements may reasonably be regarded as religious and enjoy the benefits, for example, of charitable status. On the other hand, there are those who see them as a clear indication of 'the return of the sacred' to modern society, which it was widely assumed was undergoing an inexorable process of secularization.

One thing is clear to those involved in the field of new religions: it is impossible to generalize about them. While a number do hold similar beliefs and pursue similar goals, new religions come in all shapes and sizes and are often very different from one another. That is why it is important to consider each of these religions separately before attempting to reach any overall conclusions concerning the phenomenon of new religions, and this also explains in large measure the purpose of this series.

In each book an attempt will be made to provide an objective account of a particular movement, its origins, development, beliefs, practices, aims, and appeal, and the response to it of the wider society. Some of the controversial issues surrounding these movements will also be discussed and the authors have been given the freedom to express their own opinion, based on the evidence available to them, on these matters. Technical language has been avoided wherever possible with the intention of making the series available to the widest possible readership.

PETER B. CLARKE
King's College, London

Acknowledgements

I wish to thank all those who made this book possible, especially those Rastas both black and white who answered my many questions and gave me their time and hospitality.

I would also like to thank Michael Cox, Editorial Director of The Aquarian Press, for his patience and assistance. Mrs Elsie Hinkes, who typed this manuscript, also deserves my speical thanks for her help and kindness.

None of those who assisted me, of course, is to be blamed for any error of fact or interpretation, which are entirely my own.

PETER B. CLARKE
Centre for New Religious Movements
King's College, London

Introduction
The Rastafarian Movement and New Religions in Britain

The Rastafarian movement is but one of the estimated 500 'new' religions to have emerged in Britain since 1945. Some of these religions are 'new' only in the chronological sense that in the British context they are a post-World War II phenomenon. Considered from another historical perspective and from a cultural and theological standpoint, what are referred to here as new religions — for example Hare Krishna and/or ISKCON (The International Society for Krishna Consciousness)[1] — might well be considered at the levels of doctrine and ritual as authentic developments of long established religious traditions.

The new religions in Britain derive from many different cultures and can vary enormously in terms of theological content, ritual, social composition, structure and organization, methods of recruitment, aims, attitudes towards other religions both 'new' and 'old', and towards the wider society. This makes it extremely difficult to generalize in any meaningful way about these 'new' religions. Nevertheless in the case of a large number there are certain striking similarities. Almost all of them, including the Rastafarian movement, are millenial movements prophesying in their different ways the imminent end of the present age and the establishment of a totally new dispensation. Details about precisely when and exactly how the end will come about and the form the new order will take differ from movement to movement. For the Rastafarians the present order will be razed to the ground in apocalyptic fashion around the year 2000 and then will follow, after the judgement of Babylon, oppressor of black people (see Chapter 4, pp. 45ff), a millenium of peace, justice, contentment, and happiness in Ethiopia, symbol of Africa, the 'land without Evil' (see Chapter 5, pp. 63ff).

Another characteristic that many of the new religions have in common is their emphasis on the need for knowledge leading to certitude, not simple faith. Belief in 'God', understood in a variety of different ways, is seen as inferior to knowledge or certitude. If one can come to know 'God' with absolute certitude, then why stop at the level of belief, is the question posed by many new religions. Like members of other new religions, the Rasta 'knows' Jah (God). Here 'knowing' is not, of course, the rational approach to understanding of the philosopher but something more akin to intuitive knowledge (see Chapter 5, pp. 63-4).

Moreover the aim is not only to know 'God' but even more importantly to become 'God'. As the founder of the Rajneesh movement states: 'The real . . . is to become God not to know God.' [2] One can become 'God' when one 'knows', when one is fully aware that one's inner self is divine. This is the basis of much of the theorizing about knowledge and certitude found in the new religions. In the case of the Rasta, 'Jah' is the God within who can be located and discovered by descending into the innermost recesses of one's being (see Chapter 5, pp. 64-6).

Divinizing the self is also a way of protecting one's personal identity and that of the group or race to which one belongs from social, cultural, political and other forces that are seen as threatening, even destructive. It can also be a means, as in the case of the Rastas, of re-establishing one's identity where this is perceived to have been undermined by economic exploitation and the acculturation and other demands of the host society, dominant group, or colonizing power.

Seeking the divine within the self is, moreover, an attempt to erect a bastion against the uncertainty and insecurity experienced through relying on impersonal, fragile institutions, systems and structures whose legitimacy is often questioned and whose durability is frequently put in doubt by economic factors beyond the control of any one individual, group, or country. In order to transcend the uncertainty and insecurity of the modern world and its institutions on which they have come to rely some have decided to search within themselves for security, stability, and the strength and energy to cope with doubt and uncertainty.

Reliance, then, on systems, institutions, and structures for support and security weakens, debilitates, frustrates, and results in passivity and the inability to do for oneself, to be creative. The Rastafarians themselves 'know' this from the history of the black race, a chosen race with a glorious past, that was to suffer the indignity and humiliation of the slave trade because it had ceased to do for itself and had come to rely on slaves. Africans undermined their own independence and lost their creative ability through overdependence on others. This is not their own full account, nor an historically accurate and objective explanation for the transatlantic slave trade (see Chapter 1, p. 18); but it does make the point that Rastas, along with many other adherents of new religions and seekers, see the self as divinized rather than systems, institutions and structures as the source of security and creativity.

In many cases this journey inwards to the divine, inner self is bound up not only with questions of security and creativity but also, as indicated, with the question of identity. The Rastas feel that, as individuals and as a race, the real, true identity of black people has been destroyed. Wrenched from their homeland and 'natural', normal ways of life, treated as sub-human during the era of the slave trade, and 'indoctrinated' with western values and notions and images of 'God', they must now restore their true identity by a process of deconversion and reconstruction. They must rid themselves of any idea or feeling of inferiority and decolonize their minds. This explains in part the emphasis on the divine inner nature of the self, the enthusiasm for all things African, and the glorification of the African past.

Moreover, like many other second-generation members of ethnic groups, Rastas, it would seem, are engaged on the one hand in an attempt to revitalize and preserve an old identity and on the other to forge a new one. In order to do this they have created by their rituals, language, dress, dreadlocks, and general lifestyle a sharp sense of boundary between themselves and others. No empty symbol, the tam (head-dress) in green, red, black, and yellow means allegiance to and identification with Ethiopia, symbol of an uncolonized, free and independent Africa, and a long and glorious history and civilization (see Chapters 2, 3, and 6). Such allegiance is something to be proud of after the humiliation and degradation of slavery and colonization and in a society where the sense of exile is often sharpened by discrimination.

It is perhaps the case that Rasta language, ritual, and lifestyle have become for some a barricade behind which they have retired a little too effortlessly. However, as some see the situation it was only through these means that they could restore their memory of themselves as a people and their African identity, the alternative being no meaningful history, purpose, or identity. Through their rituals, lifestyle, and music Rastas have brought their version of what it means to be African right down into their homes and on to the streets of London, Paris, New York, and other major western cities.

Rastafarian beliefs, rituals, and lifestyle have helped to provide many people of African descent with a deeper sense of their African identity. They have created a home away from home and at the same time provided some with protection from the adverse emotional and psychological effects of alienation [3] (see Chapter 7). Other religious traditions have served the same ends, for example Roman Catholicism in the context of Irish immigration to the United States, and the Ukranian Church in Canada. [4]

In the United States, as in Britain, other movements such as the Black Muslim movement have certain similarities in terms of methods and aims with the Rastafarian movement; [5] and while in one sense all of these movements may appear to operate against the development of a pluralist, multi-cultural society, they may over time nonetheless make a positive contribution to the building of such a society by providing people with the space to establish their *own* identity and on that basis interact purposefully and meaningfully with others. These movements allow people to stand outside the boundaries of the wider society, to remain at one level unassimilated and in a position to define *who* they are rather than simply having to accept a definition of themselves which others *impose* upon them. This would seem to be a necessary precondition for the emergence of a genuinely pluralist society.

While its influence has been much greater than its size would appear to warrant — there are an estimated 5,000 Rastas in Britain — it is worth pointing out that the Rastafarian movement does not necessarily represent or cater for the hopes and aspirations — religious and otherwise — of all black people in Britain, or even in Jamaica where it was founded. It is but one of the many black inspired religious movements in Britain, some of which are undoubtedly sympathetic to certain at least of the practices and aims of the Rastafarian movement.

Black Churches in Britain. There are numerous black religious organizations in contemporary Britain, some of which are in part a response to rejection and discrimination. [6] Black churches, however, are not simply the product of negative forces such as these but are also the outcome of African insight, understanding, and interpretation of the Bible, and of the conviction that to be both meaningful and universal the Christian faith has to be expressed in the symbols, rituals, and language of all peoples and cultures, including those of Africa and the Caribbean.

While there is some evidence of the existence of a Black Church in Britain in the early years of this century, [7] the development of such Churches, on a large scale dates from 1952. Since then almost 200 churches of African and Caribbean origin have been established in Britain and are attended by approximately 20 per cent of the Afro-Caribbean population. [8] Black people also attend other Christian churches, including Anglican, Roman Catholic, and United Reformed, but many tend to shun these more established institutions, often feeling unwanted or finding them uncongenial as far as the expression of their hopes and aspirations as immigrants are concerned. In Britian there has in fact been a massive defection of West Indians from the Anglican Church, which many attended regularly in the West Indies, to the Pentecostal churches, which tend to form a more effective buffer between this immigrant group and the harsh realities of life in the wider society (see Chapter 4, pp. 54-5).

Most of the West Indian Pentecostal churches are affiliated to one of several major churches, including the New Testament Church of God, the Church of God of Prophecy, and the Apostolic Church of Jesus Christ. The first of these, the New Testament Church of God, was established in Wolverhampton in 1970 by a group of West Indian Christians and today has well over a hundred separate congregations and many thousands of worshippers. While they hold to many of the same beliefs as other Pentecostal churches in Britain, West Indian Pentecostal congregations are distinguishable by their manner of worship, which involves a high level of participation by those who attend — for example, the giving of testimonies, and the extensive use of musical instruments, hand clapping, and 'shouting' during prayers.

The Aladura (praying) churches, which began life in Nigeria at the end of the First World War, are among the better known and largest of what are often referred to as the African Independent Churches to come to Britain. They include the Aladura International Church, The Brotherhood of the Cross and Star, and the Cherubim and Seraphim Church. [9] These churches, it is worth pointing out, do not regard themselves as being solely for Africans or people of African descent, but see all peoples and the whole world as their mission field. [10]

The African Methodist Episcopal Church (A.M.E.) and the African Methodist Episcopal Zion Church (A.M.E.Z.), established in North America in the early nineteenth century, have a relatively small number of mainly West Indian members in Britain. There are also several Holiness Churches in Britain — for example, the Wesleyan Holiness Church, where the majority of worshippers are West Indian. These churches separated from the North American Methodist Church in the 1840s and then contributed significantly to the rise of Pentecostalism in the United States in the nineteenth century. [11]

The Ethiopian Orthodox Church, one of the most historic branches of Christianity, is also to be found in Britain, and perhaps somewhat surprisingly has not attracted as many Rastafarians as one might have expected — perhaps because it refused to recognize the divinity of Haile Selassie, former emperor of Ethiopia and the Rastafarian messiah, and perhaps also because it is too obviously Christian. Rastafarians have expressed considerable hostility towards Christianity, especially mainstream Christianity and Roman Catholicism in particular. [12]

There is, then, in Britain a diverse, strong, and vibrant black religious life of which the Rastafarian movement, as far as its numerical size is concerned, forms only a relatively small part, but an extremely influential one nevertheless. While there are no accurate statistics for the size of its membership there are, as previously indicated, an estimated 5,000 Rastafarians in Britain. Several years ago there were an estimated 70,000 members and sympathizers in Jamaica, most of them male, working-class former Christians between the ages of eighteen and forty. [13] This reflects fairly accurately the social composition of the movement in contemporary Britain.

1

The African Diaspora

*By the waters of Babylon we sat and wept,
remembering you, O Zion.*

Psalm 137:1

Born in the ghettos of Kingston, Jamaica, the Rastafarian movement has captured the imagination of thousands of black youth, and some white youth, throughout Jamaica, the Caribbean, Britain, France, and other countries in Western Europe and North America. It is also to be found in smaller numbers in parts of Africa — for example, in Ethiopia, Ghana, and Senegal — and in Australia and New Zealand, particularly among the Maori. [1]

This highly visible religion, whose adherents wear the black, red, green, and gold woollen 'tams' covering their 'dreadlocks', has been one of the most powerful cultural forces among black youth in Jamaica and Britain in particular in recent times. It is a movement that is concerned above all else with black consciousness, with rediscovering the identity, personal and racial, of black people. There are, of course, many definitions and uses of the word identity, but here it is taken to mean broadly that which 'a person or group *is* essentially, and, as it were, permanently'. [2]

The Rastafarians 'know' that an identity exists between themselves and the ancient Israelites. Further they 'know', and confirm what they 'know', by reference to the Bible (Lamentations 4:8, 5:10; Joel 2:8; Psalm 119:83, and elsewhere) that the chosen people were black, and conclude from this that black people today are the descendants of God's elect. Moreover, the scattering and dispersal of the black race during the era of the slave trade is proof of this identity with the ancient Israelites, and like their ancestors they will return to Zion, their homeland — Ethiopia, meaning Africa.

It is to the slave trade, and colonialism and its legacy, that one must

17

turn to uncover the historical roots of the Rastas, as they are commonly known.

The transatlantic slave trade. While historians have debated at length the economic, political and social impact of the transatlantic slave trade, rather less attention has been paid to its emotional, psychological, and cultural effects on both the enslavers and the enslaved. One of the most spine-chilling and humiliating experiences imaginable is to be had from a visit to the 'Maison d'Esclaves' (House of Slaves) on the island of Gorée, just across the water from the Senegalese capital of Dakar. There, and in similar establishments along Africa's coastline, millions of Africans, packed into small dungeons, waited to be shipped across the Atlantic to a life of slavery on one of the Caribbean islands or in the Americas.

House of Slaves (Maison des Esclaves), Gorée, Senegal (*Peter Clarke*)

Estimates of the number of Africans enslaved during the era of the transatlantic slave trade (*c*.1460–*c.* 1860) vary from as low as nine million to as high as forty million. Millions of others, over a longer period of time, were taken across the Sahara and enslaved in North Africa and the Near and Middle East.[3] If we take the conservative estimate of nine million for the transatlantic slave trade, over four million of these were transported to the Caribbean islands, the largest number going to Haiti, followed by Jamaica and then Cuba.[4] A majority of those enslaved and transported to Jamaica were from the West African states of Ghana and Nigeria.

While there was some variation from one country to another in the way slaves were treated and in their socio-economic condition, all were subjected to a degrading and exploitative economic system which treated them simply as units of labour. In practice they were regarded as having no identity nor value other than in these terms.

Justifying slavery. A number of theories were advanced in justification of the slave trade, and the Rastafarians also, as we shall see, have developed their own scripturally inspired explanation of this evil. Some, among them Christian missionaries, argued that the institution of slavery was part of God's providential design for the Christianization and salvation of the African. God, it was maintained, ordained slavery as the means for raising up an African élite which, once both 'Christianized' and 'civilized', would bring in its turn both Christianity and 'civilization' to the 'dark', 'heathen' continent of Africa.[5]

It was this elect's destiny to 'cover Africa with homes and schools and Christian states' and thereby overcome 'the ignorance, animalism and barbarism of the African tribes'.[6] This was the image of Africa that not only whites but also many black Americans, Jamaicans, and others in the Caribbean internalized, accepted as authentic, and which movements such as the Rastafarian movement strive to eradicate. It also explains their tendency to mythologize and idealize the African past.

Theories justifying slavery as an institution abound in the writings of economists, lawyers, doctors, biologists, psychiatrists, anthropologists, and churchmen. Moreover, they tended to become more sophisticated from around the time of the American Declaration of Independence in 1776, when among others one of its signatories, the pioneer American psychiatrist Benjamin Rush, challenged European claims to supremacy by arguing that they were 'founded alike in ignorance and inhumanity'.[7]

While some theologians pointed to the book of Genesis to prove that blacks were the descendents of Ham, and therefore cursed, there were scholars from other disciplines who worked hard to prove on 'scientific' grounds that black and white had been separately created and that slavery could, therefore, be justified on genetic and racial grounds. In addition to the biological argument that skin pigmentation provided the basis for a scientific theory of race, other evidence was adduced from somatometry, the so-called science of comparative body measurements, which involved among other things the measurement and weighing of the brain. Blacks were presented as physiologically different from whites, not only on grounds of skin colour but also in terms of brain size, quantity of grey matter in the brain, and from every conceivable physiological and biological angle. These differences were regarded by some as irreversible, certain theologians going so far as to maintain that they had been divinely ordained. Others dismissed any attempt at racial equality through, for example, education as misguided, since this would run counter to the race trend of the African, whose vocation was to labour on the cotton and sugar plantations. This recalls the Aristotelian view that some people are slaves by nature. [8]

However, not everyone attempted to legitimate the permanent separation of the black and white races on scriptural, philosophical, and 'scientific' grounds. There were, for example, the positivists who maintained that the major differences between the races were social, economic, environmental, and cultural and that the removal of these differences could bring equality. This sort of theorizing sometimes resulted in attempts to eradicate totally all trace of black culture and institutions with a view to turning blacks into Europeans. Many black-led movements, both political and religious, including the Rastafarian movement, see acceptance and participation by blacks in such a scheme as tantamount to race suicide.

While all of this pseudo-scientific, philosophical, and theological explanation and justification of the institution of slavery and the politics of the separation of the races was taking place the slaves themselves struggled against both Church and State to regain their freedom.

The Church and slavery. The Christian churches were in practice in an especially difficult position with regard to the question of slavery. In Jamaica, the Caribbean island with which we are mainly concerned, the Anglican Church, never very large in terms of numbers of missionaries, made little or no attempt during the eighteenth century to defend the basic human rights or improve the material conditions of the slaves, or even to preach the Christian gospel to them. This was in part a consequence of this particular Church's dependence on the plantation owners, who were strongly opposed to the dissemination of Christian ideas of brotherly love, equality, and freedom. Teaching slaves to read and understand the Bible could prove to be extremely dangerous, leading to insubordination, even rebellion, and any clergyman who engaged in such an 'unacceptable' practice had to face the organized hostility of the plantation owners, who constituted a majority in the Jamaican Assembly. Paucity of clergy — some pastors had as many as 20,000 parishioners — was another reason why so little was done to instruct the slaves in the Christian faith in this period. [9]

However, these factors do not alone explain this neglect of the slave population. A number of clergyman were not only members of the ruling élite, holding civil and political offices, but also appear to have shared the views of that élite concerning the slave population. Furthermore, some of the clergy even refused to hold a service if no white person was present, while others made it their concern, no doubt to gain the approval of the plantation owners for their ministry, to ensure that the slaves continued to be peaceful, diligent, humble, and submissive to their masters. [10] Slaves, where they were instructed in the Christian faith, were encouraged to see in their condition the hand of a caring, beneficent God, transforming evil into good. As we shall see, this way of interpreting and presenting the biblical message has profoundly influenced the Rastafarian approach to the Scriptures (see Chapter 5, p. 64).

To generalize about the Christian response to slavery, as already pointed out, can give rise to distortion. In the eighteenth and early nineteenth century a number of missionary societies, in the main nonconformists such as the Moravians, Methodists, and Baptists, attempted with some success to win over the slaves to Christianity, despite the use of every means, both legal and illegal, to prevent them. These missionary societies reaped their reward when on the occasion of the emancipation in 1835 the slaves, appreciative of the efforts made on their behalf, joined these denominations in considerable numbers.

Elsewhere, for example in the American South, some nonconformist denominations, in particular the Methodists, Quakers, Presbyterians, and Baptists, made considerable efforts to convert the slaves and manifested the same opposition to slavery as was shown by their counterparts in Jamaica, although once again they met with resistance from the slaveholders. In 1784 the Methodists decided to exclude from the society any member who after a period of twelve months failed to comply with their rules for emancipation, and with certain qualifications slaveholders were refused membership unless they signed emancipation papers. [11] But the institution of slavery in the South proved too strong for those egalitarian nonconformists who strove to undermine it. Eventually compromise was necessary, the alternative being loss of all contact with the slave population. The outcome was that nonconformity fostered both rebellion and docility.

Religious meetings not only served to inculcate in the slaves the virtues of submission, obedience, and respect for property and 'lawfully' constituted authority; they also enabled them to plan and organize rebellions and to justify these by recourse to the Bible. One such slave rebellion, known as Gabriel's Rebellion, was organized in Richmond, Virginia, in 1800, where a black preacher argued that the cause of the slaves was similar to that of the Israelites and invoked God's promise that 'five of you shall conquer a hundred and a hundred a hundred thousand'.[12] The rebellion was swiftly crushed and immediately followed by the introduction of even more repressive legislation.

Religion and slave rebellions in Jamaica. As in North and South America, so also in Jamaica and the Caribbean as a whole, both the Bible and African beliefs and rituals played an important part in slave rebellions. The slaves in the Gabriel Rebellion drew on African beliefs and rituals, as well as biblical testimony, to support the insurrection and used them as a means of overcoming their oppressors. Moreover, there are examples from the African continent itself, where traditional religion was used both as an ideology and a weapon against oppression and colonial domination.[13]

In Jamaica the Maroons, most probably Spanish slaves until the English defeated Spain in 1655 and took possession of the island, had recourse to African spirits in their struggle against slavery and foreign rule, and in Jamaican history as a whole there are numerous instances of the use of African rituals, particularly of Ashanti (Ghanaian) origin, including witchcraft, exorcism and spirit possession, for the purpose of undermining slavery. The Maroons continued their resistance to English rule until March 1738, when they agreed to sign a peace treaty with the English planters. The treaty recognized Maroon rights to possess and govern their own lands, an achievement that has won for them a place of honour in Jamaican history as freedom fighers. On the other hand Rastafarians, among others, lament the fact that the Maroons agreed to abandon the struggle against foreign domination and instead decided to 'dissipate' their energies by collaborating with the English plantation owners, taking on the role of a police force.

Nonetheless slave rebellions continued, one of the most successful being in the 1831-2 insurrection led by Samuel Sharpe, probably a member of the Native Baptist Church, brought to Jamaica from the United States after the American Revolution by the slave preacher George Liele.[14] Sharpe was probably also a member of the white-led London Baptist Mission at Montego Bay. Of the slaves who joined the

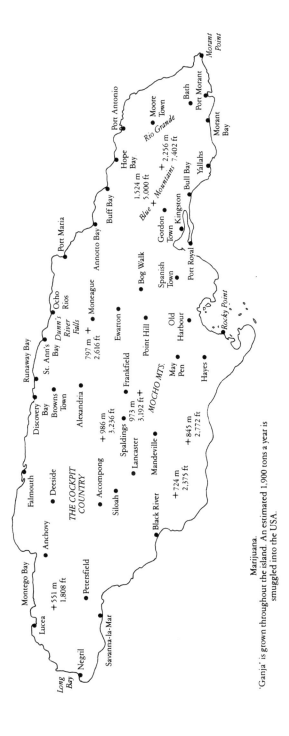

Map of Jamaica

Marijuana.
'Ganja' is grown throughout the island. An estimated 1,900 tons a year is smuggled into the USA.

rebellion a number belonged to either one or other of these Baptist Churches.

Using the Bible as his authority Sharpe spoke out vehemently against slavery, declaring that no man, whether black or white, had a right to enslave another. A charismatic leader, Sharpe convinced his followers that England had in fact already granted them their freedom and that this was withheld by the Jamaican authorities because of the opposition from the plantation owners. Sharpe then advised the slaves working on the plantations to withdraw their labour from the end of December 1831. The rebellion was to be, as far as was possible, non-violent. His followers, however, set about burning down houses and sugar works on a large plantation and this was followed by a general insurrection during which slaves in Montego Bay drove out the plantation owners and razed their property to the ground. Martial law was soon imposed and the Commander-in-Chief of the army, realizing the problems and dangers involved in such a campaign, offered an unconditional pardon to all slaves who agreed to surrender and return to their owners. Some slaves accepted only to be severely punished or put to death by their masters, but the majority took refuge in the mountains, to be hunted down by the Maroons. Thousands of slaves were slaughtered in this way, and many others were either shot or sent to the gallows.

Contemporary observers commented on the bravery and fortitude with which the slaves met their death, utterly convinced as they were of the justice of their cause. Samuel Sharpe was the last of the insurrectionists to be put to death, and in the words of one witness he 'marched to the spot where so many had been sacrificed to the demon of slavery, with a firm and even dignified step . . . clothed in a suit of new white clothes . . .'[15]

Although defeated, Sharpe and his followers contributed much towards winning the war against slavery. In 1834, within two years of Sharpe's death, slavery as an institution had been abolished throughout the British colonies, though this was only the first stage in the struggle for emancipation and freedom. Jamaica was still colonized, the planters retained almost all of their privileges, blacks were very much second-class citizens, and the island was torn by political and religious factionalism.

Further insurrections, such as the Morant Bay Rebellion of 1865, were inevitable. This rebellion was inspired and led by pastors of the Native Baptist Church of Jamaica, Paul Bogle and George William Gordon, whose aim was self-government for blacks. Though crushed by the Governor, Edward John Eyre, whose reputation for brutality is unsurpassed in the island's history, the rebellion nevertheless put an end to what amounted to rule by the plantation owners. In December 1865 Jamaica became a crown colony and the old constitution which had allowed the planters to exercise almost complete control over the destiny of the majority of the people was abolished.

Black religion and Christianity. Jamaica remained a crown colony until 1962, and for much of the nineteenth century the overwhelming majority of the legislative council were white. Moreover, until the 1920s very little could be done by the majority black population as a united political force to rectify this anomaly. Hard pressed to survive, and without effective political institutions, it was through religion and music principally that the black population expressed its hopes, aspirations, and grievances. Thus in black Jamaican history any watertight distinction between religion and politics remains an artificial one.

In the second half of the nineteenth century a number of important developments took place in Jamaican religion. The early 1860s saw an unprecedented influx of former slaves into the Christian churches, an event similar to the Great Awakening in the United States in the 1740s and which has come to be known as the Great Revival of 1860-1. This, however, did not entail a rejection of African religious beliefs and practices on the part of the converts in favour of 'authentic' Christianity. Far from it, for the converts brought as much to Christianity in the way of African insights, beliefs, and rituals as they were prepared to accept from the missionaries. They were, indeed, critical of some of the teachings, attitudes, and behaviour of some of the mission churches, resenting above all else the message of docility, submission, and obedience which these churches had once preached so loudly.

What emerged, then, from this enthusiasm for religion was not so much a thriving Christian church run on missionary lines and modelled on European institutions but the growth of African Christianity which took a number of different forms. Some of the sects and cults that came into existence, such as Pukkumina, adopted in the main African beliefs and rituals; others, like Revival, were as much African as Christian in these respects; yet others, for example Revival Zion, were mostly Christian in outlook.[16] All, nonetheless, practised spiritual healing, and Revival movements were organized along similar lines with shepherds exercising varying degrees of authority over a band or group of believers who assembled for worship in what are commonly known as yards. In some cases the yard took on the character of a commune, in others it amounted to no more than a meeting place hallowed by a shrine. In addition to healing, worship would normally include drumming and chanting, counselling, and spirit possession.

The religious situation in Jamaica was further intensified with the arrival of increasing numbers of Pentecostalist missionaries from the United States from the early years of this century, reaching a climax in the 1920s. These Pentecostalist churches — The Church of God, The Church of God in Christ, The Apostolic Faith, and many others — attracted large numbers from the missionary churches; like the Afro-Christian Revivalist sects they laid great emphasis on healing, baptism in the spirit, glossolalia (speaking in tongues), and exorcism, and their services, in which use was made of folk instruments, hand clapping and chanting, bore a close resemblance to those of the Revivalist movements.

There were, however, significant differences between Pentecostalists and Revivalists, the former laying far more emphasis on the centrality of the Bible, on baptism in the Spirit as the only form of spirit possession, and on the necessity for a strict, puritanical lifestyle involving abstention from alcohol and tobacco. The Revivalists for their part attached as much signifance to dreams and visions as channels of divine revelation as to the Bible and allowed for spirit possession by angels, ancestors, and every kind of spirit, both good and evil. In general their approach to life was less governed by rules of an ascetic, puritanical nature.

These religious movements provided a means for people with few, if any, effective political institutions, of expressing their hopes, fears, and aspirations. With the history of slavery embedded in their memories, and still denied any real participation in the political process, many black Jamaicans turned to Revivalist, Pentecostalist, and nonconformist churches for their centre of gravity.

Meanwhile a black Jamaican 'prophet' had emerged in the person of Marcus Garvey, who proclaimed loud and clear that the only centre of gravity for black people was Africa and promised them that if they returned there they would enjoy a collective salvation that would be both immediate and total. This promise was to capture the imagination of many black people in the United States and has become a central 'tenet' of the Rastafarian movement. Garvey's proclamations and plans for repatriation to Africa, and those of the Rastafarians, need to be seen against the background of the nineteenth-century Back-to-Africa movement and the rise of Ethiopianism as an ideology for change.

2

The Back-to-Africa Movement and the Rise of Ethiopianism

Princes shall come out of Egypt;
Ethiopia shall soon stretch forth
her hands to God.

Psalm 68:31

The idea of returning to Africa and the concept of Ethiopianism are two fundamental ingredients of Rastafarian ideology. Throughout history there have been numerous examples of peoples driven from their homelands or forced to migrate for one reason or another and who have sought to return. In exile their homeland often takes on the character of a sacred place, a promised land, a land without evil. In Jamaica, the Caribbean as a whole, and the Americas the lore of Africa figured prominently in the daily life of the slaves and their dependents; and as we have seen, religion was often the most effective means of keeping in contact with African customs, culture and history. From the Bible also they discovered, they believed, a great deal about themselves, their history, and their homeland.

While Marcus Garvey (1887–1940), and after him the Rastafarians, have been the most vigorous champions of the Back-to-Africa movements, certainly this century, the movement did not begin with them. Nor did the ideology of Ethiopianism, which not only gave hope for the future but served also to focus the minds of Africans on the former achievements of Africans in Africa.

In the late eighteenth century and during the nineteenth century movements emerged advocating the return of Africans to Africa. The idealists who supported this scheme had visions of progressive, Christian nations arising on that continent. This vision of a regenerated, Christianized, 'civilized' Africa was present amongst late eighteenth-century British evangelicals and humanitarians and the founding of Sierra Leone colony in 1787 was the first attempt to give concrete form and content to this ideal. The founders of Sierra Leone hoped that the settlement would become the centre from which Christianity and 'legitimate' trade would spread to the rest of Africa through the agency of Africans who had received the benefits of the Christian faith and 'civilization'.[1] Among the first settlers were an estimated 377 poor blacks from Britain, followed in 1792, by 1,131 others from Nova Scotia. In 1800, 500 Maroons from Jamaica were resettled in Sierra Leone.

In North America as well schemes were devised to enable emancipated slaves to return to their original homeland, leading to the establishment of Liberia as a self-governing independent state. As early as 1773 Samuel Hopkins, pastor of the First Congregational Church of Newport, Rhode Island, proposed a voluntary plan to return freed Christian slaves to Africa for the purpose of evangelizing the continent. There was also a deep interest in emigration among the Afro-American community in New England.

In 1808 Paul Cuffee, a New England trader and owner of a small fleet of ships, became, as far as it is known, the first black American in the United States to champion the cause of repatriation. He, likewise, wanted to build a black Christian nation in Africa and replace slave trading with 'legitimate' commerce. Like many other blacks, he was also motivated by racial pride. Cuffee sought to demonstrate to the white world that the African people were not 'slaves by nature' but had all the talents required to establish a flourishing nation equal to any other. Cuffee transported 38 black Americans to Sierra Leone in December 1815, but his activities came to an abrupt end with his death in 1817. Meanwhile, organizations such as the American Colonization Society, founded in December 1816, undertook to transport black Americans to Africa, though it met with considerable opposition, especially from the black community who quickly realized that it could be used simply as a means of getting rid of them.

The colonization of Africa by emancipated blacks was undoubtedly seen in certain quarters as the solution to a number of interrelated problems. For some it was one possible way of preventing miscegenation. As Thomas Jefferson expressed it: 'Among the Romans emancipation required but one effort. The slave when free might mix without staining the blood of the master. But with us a second step is necessary unknown to history. When freed he is to be removed beyond the reach of mixture.'[2] Others maintained that a free black population was a serious danger to the peace and stability of the nation, and therefore promoted the cause of colonization. In Britain there were those who regarded the Sierra Leone project as part of the solution to the socio-economic problem of the black poor in the major cities.

Although many blacks opposed the colonization scheme there were others, among them clergymen, who gave it their unqualified support. The latter, further, sought to arouse the interests of black Americans in missionary work in Africa. They preached widely throughout the country to black audiences, expounding the theory of Providential Design which they hoped would persuade their listeners to return to Africa as Christian missionaries. Some black Americans did take up the challenge and fulfil their destiny by returning to Africa, mainly to Liberia, as missionaries; like their European counterparts, they did all in their power to eradicate African beliefs, rituals, customs, and culture in the name of Christianity and 'civilization'. But not all took a purely negative view of Africa, nor for that matter an entirely positive view of Christianity, as is evidenced in the writings and activities of one of the greatest advocates of pan-Africanism, Edward Wilmot Blyden (1832-1912), precursor of Marcus Garvey.

Edward Wilmot Blyden and the Back-to-Africa movement. Blyden was born in 1832 on the Danish occupied island of St Thomas in the West Indies, of Ibos parents from eastern Nigeria. [3] In 1850 he travelled to the United States, where he hoped to become a student at Rutgers Theological College with a view to becoming a pastor in the Dutch Reformed Church. Rutgers, however, refused him admission, as did two other theological colleges, because of the colour of his skin. Blyden then met a group of prominent Presbyterians associated with the American Colonization Society who informed him about Liberia and the hopes they entertained of creating out of this 'dark', 'barbarous' and 'heathen' land — a view of Africa, incidentally, which Blyden at this stage accepted without question — a new and progressive civilization.

Blyden showed great enthusiasm for these plans and wanted to extend them to cover not only Liberia but also 'the dark regions of Ashantee [in modern day Ghana] and Dahomey [the present day Peoples' Republic of Benin] and bring those barbarous tribes under civilized and enlightened influences'. [4] He arrived in Monrovia, capital of Liberia, in 1851 and was to have an important influence on developments in West Africa for over half a century thereafter as a clergyman, educationalist, writer, and statesman. According to one scholar, Blyden was the only one in West Africa to see the problem posed for Africans by western influences in their entirety and 'who tried and succeeded in fashioning a total philosophy of African-ness which not only had great appeal for his contemporaries but for future generations of Africans as well'. [5] According to the same historian it was Blyden 'who re-established the psychic and emotional sense of security of the African in the face of Europe's intrusion with a brilliance that foreshadowed to a remarkable degree African thinking in the mid-20th century when another generation of Africans achieving political independence from Europe, sought economic and cultural independence as well'. [6] Whether they claim him as such or not, the Rastafarians have in Blyden a founding father.

Among other things Blyden wrote a considerable amount in vindication of the black race. He emphasized above all in his writings on this question that the black race could be proud of its past achievements; that African institutions, traditions, and customs were sound and valuable and with some modifications should be preserved; that black people had special inherent qualities and attributes which they should strive to develop and project and in this way develop to the full their distinctive 'African personality'. [7] And though a Christian clergyman he also maintained that Christianity, more so than Islam, tended not only to retard this development but even to place almost insuperable obstacles in its way. [8] All of these themes figure prominently in Rastafarian thinking.

With regard to Africa's achievements Blyden pointed to the Pyramids and wrote: 'This, thought I, was the work of my African progenitors . . . Feelings came over me far different from those I have ever felt when looking at the mighty works of European genius. I felt that I had a peculiar heritage in the Great Pyramid built by the enterprising sons of Ham, from which I descended. The blood seemed to flow faster in my veins. I seemed to hear the echo of those illustrious Africans . . . could my voice have reached every African in the world, I would have earnestly addressed him . . . "Retake your Fame"'. [9] Though the style might jar a little there is much here that would appeal to any Rastafarian, and this is equally true of what Blyden had to say about Ethiopia.

Using as his main sources the Hebrew version of the Bible, Herodotus, and Homer, Blyden moved on from his discussion of the contribution of Africans to the ancient civilization of Egypt to point to the achievements in the fields of learning and culture of the Ethiopians, who represented 'the highest rank of knowledge and civilization. [10] He also pointed out that early Christian theology was shaped and moulded by Tertullian, Cyprian, and St Augustine — all of them Africans — and noted that much of the political, commercial, and agricultural history of the Americas is the history of the black race. [11]

On the question of race Blyden would be regarded by many today as being on shaky ground. He was to some extent influenced by the ideas propounded by Gobineau, who in his *Essay on the Inequality of the Races* maintained that there was a hierachy of races with the

African race near to or at the bottom. Though Blyden did not accept this proposition, arguing instead that each race was equal but different, he endorsed the view that there are innate and permanent differences in the moral and mental endowments of races, each one having its own 'talents', 'instincts', and 'energies'. And while he did not accept the opinion that it was race rather than environment or circumstance that provided the key to the understanding of the history of a people he does appear to have held that there exists 'an instinctive antipathy among races', and that the mixing of races was an obstacle to nation building. [12]

According to Blyden the distinctive qualities and attributes of the black race were sympathy, cheerfulness, a willingness to serve and, most important of all, its spirituality. This was something far more important than technology or material well-being, and as the 'spiritual conservatory of the world' Africa could contribute more than anywhere else to the peace and stability of human civilization, continually threatened by the materialism and destructive scientific inventions of the white race. [13]

Blyden's views of the African appear to bear a striking resemblance to Rousseau's 'noble savage'. His understanding of Africa's destiny was equally romantic, although no less so than Mazzini's of Italy, or Karamanzin's or Dostoevsky's of Russia. But it is important to keep in mind what Blyden was attempting to achieve, and the same applies when examining Rastafarian views on African personality and Africa's role in history. Blyden was seeking as much as anything else to dispel what he regarded as false notions and myths then in wide circulation about Africa as the 'dark', 'heathen', 'uncivilized' continent which had contributed nothing to human civilization and which had nothing African, and therefore 'unique', to offer mankind. He also sought to re-educate Africans about their past, to eradicate any belief or feeling of inferiority. And, just as important, he was searching for a viable solution to the thorny and complex problem created by the contact between western, industrialized, increasingly secular and technologically oriented cultures and those of Africa, the heartland of that wisdom which derives from its 'inherently spiritual understanding' and approach to life.

Blyden further, like many Rastafarians today, saw a parallel between the history of the black race and that of the Jews. Both peoples, he believed, were united by a history of dispersion, intense humiliation, and suffering. This, however, was all part of a divine plan. The Jewish longing for their homeland was, he believed, no different from that of millions of Africans scattered throughout the world, and he was to remind the Jews that Moses, the great prophet and legislator who had delivered Israel from the house of bondage, was an African by birth, and also encouraged them to come and share Africa with the Africans. [14]

The return to Africa of Africans was a constant preoccupation of Blyden's, as was his concern for a greater appreciation of African culture, customs, and institutions. He stressed that it was in Africa and in African history that the soul of the African race was to be found, and that it was to these sources, and not to European or American civilization, that Africans ought to go for inspiration for the future. In support of this he wrote:

> Love of race will take possession of the cultivated Negro; and the enforced consciousness under which he has been labouring, of oneness with the Anglo-Saxon, will be extinguished. Under no other circumstances can he be properly developed. Love of race must be the central fire to heat all his energies . . . Hitherto the Negro overshadowed by a foreign and powerful people . . . many of the elements of true manhood could not be developed. [15]

Another staunch advocate of the theory that it was only in Africa that an African could realize his potential to the full was the black Harvard-trained physician Martin R. Delaney. He visited Liberia and Nigeria in 1859 and while there was strongly critical of the Christian missionaries who gave their African converts new names at baptism, maintaining that this would lead to a loss of identity. Along with Blyden, Delaney was one of the first to use the slogan 'Africa for the Africans', believing that it was only in Africa that Africans could preserve their identity. [16]

Once again there is in all of this much that is Rastafarian, as there is in Blyden's view of African institutions such as polygamy. He defended polygamy, which was under attack from Christian missionaries in particular, on the grounds that it was an important means of ensuring that 'the functional work of sex was not abused', and of enabling all women to share naturally and normally in this work, contributing thereby to a 'healthy posterity and unfailing supply of population'. [17]

Blyden, though perhaps less trenchant in his criticism of Christianity than some Rastafarians, nevertheless accused it of similar errors and distortions with regard to Africans. It had inculcated, he maintained, a sense of inferiority, an attitude of acceptance and submissiveness. Furthermore, by condemning and outlawing African customs and institutions it alienated Africans, in a way Islam did not, from themselves and their own culture; as a consequence their memory as a people had been lost. Blyden, as we have seen, was a Christian

Map of Africa

clergyman, whose purpose was not to condemn Christianity for the sake of it but rather to encourage it to adapt to the African condition. He admired Islam for this, and attributed much of its success to the fact that it had allowed itself to be domesticated and indigenized while Christianity, much as he wanted it to be even more successful, placed a barrier between itself and African culture.

Christianity was also bound up with the transatlantic slave trade, as indeed Islam was with the trans-Saharan trade, and had failed in Blyden's view to break those chains and set the African free. Nevertheless, despite his misgivings about Christianity's performance, Blyden, along with other African clergymen like the Nigerian bishop James Johnson, wanted to see the establishment of a Christian theocracy in Africa that would embrace the entire continent and be controlled and managed by Africans. This aspiration was grounded, at least in part, in what we have already referred to as the ideology of Ethiopianism.

Ethiopianism. In the writings of Blyden there is frequent reference to Egypt and Ethiopia, to the remarkable civilizations they created, and to biblical passages in which they are mentioned. The main purpose here was to demonstrate that Africans were not inferior to any other race, that they had not been destined by God to be the slaves for all time of any other race, but were, on the contrary, special, a favoured race; for did not the Psalmist foretell that 'Princes shall come out of Egypt; Ethiopia shall soon stretch forth her hands to God' (Psalm 68:31)?

Biblical references such as this underlay the development of Ethiopianism as a dynamic mythology in the Caribbean and in many parts of Africa. Ethiopia as a term became synonymous with Africa and Africa was projected as the mother of all civilizations. Ethiopianism, however, was not simply a backward looking ideology, for while it encouraged black people to feel pride in their past, it also pointed to a glorious future when Ethiopia, meaning Africa, would rise up again as the Psalmist had predicted. African nationalists, among them Blyden, not only romanticized and eulogized the achievements of the black race: they also spoke of the day when that race would become the model for all others.

Ethiopianism expressed itself in a variety of ways. In South Africa in the last quarter of the nineteenth century it found expression in the form of an independent church movement. Out of this movement emerged many 'Ethiopian' churches as they have come to be known, one of the earliest and largest being that established in Pretoria in 1892 by the black South African Mangena N. Mokone.[18] Familiar with Psalm 68:31, Mokone, a former Wesleyan minister, named his church the Ethiopian Church and interpreted the psalm to mean that God intended Africans to be the leaders of the Church in Africa, an intention ignored by Europeans.

The Ethiopian churches established in South Africa were part of an attempt by black people to acquire freedom, responsibility for their own affairs, and the right to express their own personality and preserve their own identity in their own society, which was now largely under foreign control. And in this context the use of the term Ethiopian to describe these churches was most apt since Ethiopia was an independent state where Africans were in control of their own destiny.

In the rise then of the Ethiopian churches we have, as in Jamaica and elsewhere during the era of slavery, another example of the use of the Bible to legitimate two diametrically opposed interest groups and ideologies. On the one hand, in the case of the blacks, it opened up, in the form of the biblical Ethiopia, the vision of a homeland and of a golden past, revitalizing the hopes and aspirations of an oppressed people. And on the other, we see it being used to legitimate foreign domination, exploitation, and oppression.

Literally thousands of Ethiopian churches were to spring up not only in South Africa but also in many parts of sub-Saharan Africa during the colonial era. Some of them took the form of national religions, asserting strongly that Africa should be ruled by Africans. They were in fact at the forefront of the early nationalist movement. As one historian points out, the first Nigerian nationalists looked upon themselves as Ethiopians and as early as the 1860s were making use of the Ethiopian slogan 'Africa for the Africans'. [19]

In Jamaica itself, the home of the Rastafarian movement, the concept of Ethiopianism can be traced back even further. In 1784 George Liele, the American Baptist preacher and ex-slave, named the first Baptist Church on the island the Ethiopian Baptist Church. During the time of slavery in Jamaica, North America, and elsewhere, the notion of Ethiopia, like the story of Israel's exodus from Egypt with which they identified, helped the slaves to project a future radically different from the present. In the same way Old Testament prophecies of the destruction of Israel's enemies, as one writer points out, 'easily and naturally fitted the slaves' desire that whites should suffer just retribution for the brutality of slavery'. [20]

Today the concept of Ethiopianism and the Back-to-Africa movement, with certain modifications, differences in interpretation and emphasis, live on in the Rastafarian movement and this, rather than large scale repatriation to Africa, is the legacy not only of Blyden but also of other black spokesmen like the Jamaican Marcus Garvey, often referred to as 'black Moses', whose Back-to-Africa movement, prophecies, inspirational writings, and speeches have earned for him something akin to the status of a prophet among Rastafarians.

3

Marcus Garvey:
Black Moses and Prophet
of the God of Ethiopia

*Look to Africa when a black King shall be
crowned for the day of deliverance is near.*

Prophecy attributed to Marcus Garvey.

The Back-to-Africa movement of the nineteenth century enjoyed little
success and left Blyden, among others, looking forward to the day when
a black Moses would arise to lead black Americans, and all black people
dispersed during the era of the slave trade, back to Africa. Blyden wrote:
'The Negro leader of the Exodus who will succeed will be a Negro of
the Negroes, like Moses was a Hebrew of the Hebrews — even if
brought up in Pharaoh's palace he will be found. No half Hebrew and
half Egyptian will do the work . . . for this work heart, soul and faith
are needed.'[1]

Although he did not succeed in bringing about the actual physical
repatriation of black people in the United States and elsewhere to
Africa, Marcus Garvey, the charismatic black Jamaican leader,
organized and led the first genuine black mass movement in America
and Europe, the principal aim of which was the return of Africans to
Africa. And if this return is understood, as some Rastafarians
understand it, in other than a purely physical sense, for example as
intellectual, psychological, and emotional return, or a fuller awareness
and consciousness of being African, a return at the level of identity,
then Garvey achieved a great deal. Through his militant Universal
Negro Improvement Association (U.N.I.A.), Garvey, in the opinion
of one observer, 'awakened a race consciousness that made Haarlem
felt around the world'.[2]

Garvey was not the only West Indian in the United States to attempt
to launch a Back-to-Africa movement in the first quarter of this century.
The Barbadian Dr Albert Thorne tried for a quarter of a century,
beginning in 1897, to effect the colonization of Central Africa by black

Americans.[3] Thorne was convinced that Africa was the only place in the world where black people would be respected as a race, a conviction shared, as we have seen, by Blyden, Delaney, Garvey, and by Rastafarians in general.

In the early 1920s it was Garvey who possibly exercised the greatest influence on blacks in America, and perhaps also on those in Europe. Kwame Nkrumah, nationalist leader and first President of independent Ghana (formerly the Gold Coast), and a student in the United States during the Garvey campaign, gives a glimpse of the tremendous impact made by the Jamaican on blacks in North America. Nkrumah wrote:

> I concentrated on finding a formula by which the whole colonial question and the problem of imperialism could be solved. I read Hegel, Marx, Engels, Lenin and Mazzini. The writings of these men did much to influence me in my revolutionary ideas and activities . . . but I think of all the literature I studied the book that did more than any other to fire my enthusiasm was *Philosophy and Opinions of Marcus Garvey* . . . Garvey with his philosophy of 'Africa for the Africans' and his 'Back to Africa' movement did much to inspire the Negroes of America in the 1920s.[4]

Later, it should be mentioned, Nkrumah was to disavow Garvey's philosophy of Africa for the Africans.[5]

The Garvey movement, like the Rastafarian movement, was born perhaps as much from despair of ending injustice and discrimination in America as it was from a vision of Africa as a 'Land without Evil'. In the words of Gunnar Myrdal, this movement 'tells of a dissatisfaction so deep that it amounts to a hopelessness of ever gaining a full life in America'.[6]

Garvey was motivated above all else by the belief that there was more hope for black Americans if, by becoming fully aware of their African identity and destiny, they felt inspired to build a future in their own homeland. He felt strongly the need not only to demonstrate the greatness of the African past, which he believed the prejudiced eye of the white man had overlooked, but also to place Africa on a par with other nations in the contemporary world by laying the foundations for a collective African initiative with a view to advancing the quality of life and standard of living of the people of that continent.

This notion of returning to Africa to be uplifted by and to uplift the continent was one that many black Americans entertained and acted upon in the period under discussion, but the underlying reasoning was not always the same. For example, the black bishop of the Methodist Episcopal Church, Henry Turner, passionately insisted, like Garvey, that returning to Africa was the only way for black Americans to achieve salvation, that it was the only place in the world where talented young blacks could better themselves economically, and establish their own government. But unlike Garvey, who believed there was little to be gained by implanting a Western version of Christianity in Africa, Turner saw in repatriation a means of doing precisely this, of building 'a centre of Christian civilization that will help redeem the land of our ancestry'.[7]

In 1891, on a visit to Sierra Leone, Turner spoke of being 'crazy with delight' on finally getting to Africa, of being highly impressed with the cleanliness and progressive appearance of the capital, Freetown, and of his surprise at the 'decency' of the African.[8] Like many others Turner had been brought up to regard Africa as the 'dark', 'heathen', 'unenlightened' continent in need of moral regeneration. He wrote numerous articles in his newspaper, *The Voice of Africa* encouraging black Americans to return as missionaries, reminding them that 'These are our folk. We all came from that stock.'[9] Turner, however, did not see anything positive coming out of Africa itself.

Adopting what was a variation of the theory of Providential Design, he maintained that God had willed that Africans be brought to America as slaves in order that they might come into contact both with Christian civilization and the powerful white race, and thereby be ready to return to their homeland to make it 'what the white man had made of Europe and America'.[10] He even advocated that a modified form of slavery be reinstituted, whereby Africans would be sold to whites for a period of seven years and then returned to Africa 'raised to a plane of civilization that would be a blessing to them'.[11] This is not the Rastafarian line, nor was it the position adopted by Garvey.

Marcus Garvey stepped into the United States with a ready made programme, outlined in the manifesto of the Universal Negro Improvement Association and African Committees League, founded in Jamaica in August 1914. The Association's main aims as expressed in the manifesto were repatriation to Africa, the creation of African independent states, and the engendering of pride of race. In 1920 at its convention in New York the U.N.I.A. drew up a 'Declaration of the Rights of Negro Peoples of the World', which spelt out these aims in greater detail and called, like Blyden and Delaney, for 'Africa for the Africans at home and abroad'.[12]

Garvey frequently returned in his speeches and writings to the themes of Africa for the Africans, of pride not shame in a black skin, and to a defence of black history. He wrote:

But when we come to consider the history of man was not the Negro, was he not great once? Yet honest students of history can recall the day when Egypt, Ethiopia and Timbuctoo towered in their civilization, towered above Europe, towered above Asia, when Europe was inhabited by a race of cannibals, a race of savages, of naked men, heathens and pagans, Africa was peopled with a race of cultured black men, who were cultured and refined; men who it is said, were like gods. [13]

This line of argument could prove, of course, to be counter-productive in the struggle for African freedom and independence, and indeed wherever colonial rule had been established. This was appreciated by, for example, Nigerian and Indian nationalists, who stressed that illiteracy, poverty, and low technological development were not in themselves indicators of a lack of wisdom, sophistication, and refinement, or of the ability to govern. [14] Nonetheless Garvey inspired many by his defence of black history and civilization and in his creation of a 'new ideal' for Africans in the form of the black God.

The God of Ethiopia. 'We Negroes', Garvey wrote, 'have found a new ideal. Whilst our God has no colour, yet it is human to see everything through our own spectacles, and since the white people have seen their God through white spectacles, we have now started out, late though it be to see our God through our own spectacles. The God of Isaac and the God of Jacob, let them exist for the race that believes in the God of Isaac and the God of Jacob. We Negroes believe in the God of Ethiopia, the everlasting God — God the son, God the Holy Ghost, the one God of all ages. That is the God in whom we believe but we shall worship Him through the spectacles of Ethiopia.' [15]

Garvey was not the first black person to react in this way to the image of God as, in his view, it was presented to the African by western Christianity. Black slaves in South America had spoken of Christianity as the white man's religion, and in many parts of Africa one encounters the same response. In Nigeria, for example, from the late nineteenth century, there was a growing tendency to oppose the introduction of what had come to be regarded as the white man's version of God, and of religion. As one Nigerian expressed it in the early years of this century, 'British Christianity teaches the superiority of the white man to the black, while God teaches equality and the right of every nation to become a holy nation.' He added: 'No nation has the right to say to another, worship God after my own fashion, sing to God in my own tune, say my own prayers, speak to God in my own language, marry after my own fashion . . .' [16] 'To worship a foreign God in a foreign church planted in Africa, to follow foreign customs and ideas, to adopt foreign names and habits . . .', explained another Nigerian, 'is nothing more than race suicide . . . We are thus justified in calling into existence an African church independent of foreign aid and control.'[17] According to this view, then, each nation or race has the right and duty to create its own religion, to have its own messiah or messiahs, and by accepting a foreign religion, a nation or a people forfeits both its identity and soul.

Although he was not the originator of the concept of a black God Garvey articulated this and related ideas in the North American context with a sharpness and directness that were unprecedented. He was struggling to create at every level — political, social, cultural, and religious — a world with which black Americans, and indeed black people everywhere, could identify. As the world was, black people outside Africa had nothing, not even an interpretation and understanding of themselves and God, which they could call their own. They, and everything they did, and the world in which they lived, were defined by white people, and thus in Garvey's view what was urgently needed was a history, a state, a passport other than the colour of their skin, and a God of their own.

In the sphere of religion Garvey's determination to relate to God in an African way resulted in the establishment in 1921 of the African Orthodox Church with the Antiguan George Alexander McGuire, an Episcopal clergyman living in Boston, as its first black American bishop. This church had a considerable influence on independent African churches in South and East Africa. McGuire attempted to destroy completely the conventional association of the colour white with God, Christ, and all that was 'good', and black with the devil and all that was 'evil'. Thus at the U.N.I.A. Convention in August 1924 he appealed to black Americans to burn any pictures of white Christs and white Madonnas and encouraged them to provide 'a black Madonna and a black Christ for the training of our children'.[18] He also declared that from henceforth the devil and 'evil' would be characterized and symbolized by black people as white. Very few Garveyites, let alone black Americans, joined the African Orthodox Church or supported the idea of a new black religion. And the same was true of Canada, where the church established a branch in Sydney, British Columbia, in 1921, and ministered to the needs of the West Indies working in the steel mills. However, only a very small percentage of Canadian-born black people joined the church.

Garvey's ideas influenced other black movements in the United States, for example the Divine Peace Mission led by Fr Divine, the Black Muslim and the Black Jewish cults. The Peace Mission according to one observer 'was run by blacks under a black God',[19] while Elijah Muhammad, an officer and later 'prophet' of the Nation of Islam organization, acknowledged his great debt to Garvey. Many Garveyites, further, joined the Moorish American Science Temple of Noble Drew Ali; and a number of black Jewish leaders such as Arnold Ford from Barbados derived much of their inspiration from Garvey, emphasizing in their preaching that black Jews were Ethiopian Hebrews, or Falashas, who had been deprived of their name and religion during the era of the slave trade, and that Jesus was black. One of them reportedly would wave a picture of a white Jesus before his congregation and ask 'Who the hell is this? Nobody knows! They say it's Jesus! That's a damned lie. Jesus was black.'[20]

When Garveyism collapsed as a movement in the late 1920s the trend set of visualizing God as black or African continued on in the Black Jewish and Black Muslim movements, and was to be taken up by Rastafarians. But for Garvey, as for the Rastafarian, the solution to the black person's problem lay as much in establishing a black nation as it did in fashioning an image of God that black people could identify with, worship without feeling alien and inferior, and use to fulfil their God-given destiny, which consisted in bringing to the world 'the sense of justice, the sense of equity, the sense of charity that would make men happy and God satisfied'.[21] No other race could perform this task. In this way Garvey attempted to discourage black people in white, advanced, modern society from believing that 'progress' had left them behind, from thinking that they had no special, unique contribution to make to the progress and well-being of mankind.

'Ethiopia, thou Land of our fathers . . .'   In the manifesto of the U.N.I.A. Garvey wrote that one of the principal aims of the movement was 'to establish a central nation for the race, where they will be given the opportunity to develop themselves . . .'[22] While others, both black and white Americans, encouraged black people to remain in the United States, seen as their true homeland, and to struggle for recognition and equality of opportunity there, Garvey consistently opposed this idea. Indeed he expressed greater sympathy and support for the militantly anti-black, racialist approach of the Ku Klux Klan, established in 1915, than for such an idea, which he dismissed as an attempt to appeal to the black person's 'vanity and not to his good common sense'.[23]

There would always exist, he believed, prejudice between black and white in the United States as long as the white population continued to regard the former as intruders, 'so long as white labourers believe that black labourers are taking their jobs; so long as white artisans believe that black artisans are performing the work that they should do . . . so long as white politicans believe that black politicans and statesmen are seeking the same positions in the nation's government . . .'[24]

Garvey insisted that self-fulfilment and self-realization would never be possible for the black person outside of Africa and the summer of 1919, known as 'Red Summer', in which there were twenty-six race riots in the United States, did much to convince some waverers that he was right. Garvey even appealed to the conscience of liberal white America to help him convey the truth of this message to black people. He then set about offering a glimpse of black people holding power in a black nation. At the 1920 U.N.I.A. convention in Haarlem, Garvey was appointed the provisional president of Africa and proceeded to appoint ministers. Orders, such as the Knight of the Nile and the Distinguished Service Order of Ethiopia, were conferred, and a flag in the Ethiopian colours of red (for the blood of the race), black (for the skin of the race), and green (for the hope of a new life in Africa) was unfurled, while the convention sang the new national anthem: 'Ethiopia, thou land of our Fathers'.[25]

In Ethiopia, and only there, Garvey was convinced, would black people be able to give evidence of their own ability and of their own special talents. There would no longer be any necessity to ape white people, to accept alien leadership, ideas, and ideals. The legacy of slavery, which continued to hold back the African emotionally, psychologically, socially, economically, politically and in every conceivable way, would be finally cast aside.

The collapse of the Garvey movement.   Garvey's Back-to-Africa movement, his black nationalism, often referred to as a form of 'Black Zionism', was as much as anything an attempt to decolonize social, moral, and ethical values and to establish a basic, distinctive African personality and identity. It was also very much concerned with the related issue, already mentioned, of the right to self-definition, a right that implies the freedom, means and space not only to define who one is, but also to originate perspectives, to interpret the meaning of history, of life, and of day-to-day events.

All of this is part of Rastafarian thinking and is expressed and symbolized in their bearing, the clothes they wear, their hair style, lifestyle, beliefs, and rituals. Black people, Garvey was persuaded, had been for too long the 'victims' of white definitions of who they were and what they should become; what was called for if the situation was to change was a revolution in black people's awareness and consciousness of themselves, a revolution that to some extent involved the demonization of whites. The ideal setting for this transformation was Africa.

Looked at in this way it is difficult to assess how successful the Garvey movement was. He was but one of a number of black leaders pressing for greater self-awareness, self-reliance, and race pride among black people. The contribution of others like Blyden, the pioneer of the black history movement, Thorne, Turner, and Delaney have already been discussed. There were also others, for example the militant black Americans Carter G. Woodson and W. E. B. Du Bois, the pioneer Pan-Africanist, along with the West Indian barrister H. Sylvester Williams, a moving spirit behind the first ever Pan-African Conference held in London in 1900. It was at this conference that Du Bois made the far-sighted and by now famous statement that: 'The problem of the Twentieth Century is the colour line.'[26] It was Du Bois also, as one historian has pointed out, who in 'The African Roots of War', an important article on the First World War, anticipated Lenin's thesis on the colonial origins of that war.[27]

Other black Americans, for example Brooker T. Washington, Ghanaians, among them Hayford, Aggrey, Nkrumah, Nigerians, for example Majola Agbebi whose declaration 'I am a negro and all negro. I am black all over, and proud of my beautiful black skin', expressed concisely and pointedly all that the Négritude movement ever wanted to express, all of these, and more, contributed in different ways to the awakening and articulation of a race consciousness among black people in Africa, the Caribbean, the United States, and Europe. They also had a considerable impact on the development of an emerging African nationalism, and most of all perhaps on its cultural and ideological dimension.[28]

Garveyism, although organizationally and institutionally a separate entity, and with its own policies and brand of black consciousness and black nationalism, was only one movement, albeit an important one, among many overlapping black-led movements promoting the ideas of black self-reliance and independence and of a separate black identity and personality.

The Depression, paradoxically, focused the attention of many black Americans on the situation in the United States and contributed to a decline in their interest in Africa. This was the context in which Garveyism as an organization began to lose its way and disintegrate. Garvey's own personal misfortunes did nothing to help matters. Not only did he have to contend with considerable hostility from Du Bois, among others, he was also fined 1,000 dollars and sentenced to five years in prison in Atlanta in 1925, after being charged with 'fraudulent representations' and 'deceptive artifices' in connection with the sale of stock of his Black Star steamship line, whose ships were meant to be a symbol of the enterprise and hopes of the black race. The trial in fact, while it showed incompetence, did not prove any criminal intent to defraud.

Garvey also met with opposition from the Liberian government and this as much as anything else wrecked his Back-to-Africa movement. Liberia wanted only a few useful immigrants, not the millions Garvey intended to help repatriate. After his release from prison in 1927 — his sentence having been commuted — Garvey was deported to Jamaica, where he tried with very little success to revive the U.N.I.A. When he moved to London in 1935 there were only a few small groups of Garveyites in Jamaica, and it was these that kept alive his ideas of 'Africa for the Africans, those at home and abroad', attributed to him prophetic pronouncements concerning the advent of a black messiah, and came to honour him as a black prophet.

Prior to Garvey's death in London in January 1940 the Rastafarian movement, the most recent of the Back-to-Africa movements, had already been born, and while it rejected some of Garvey's methods there can be no doubt that as far as its goal is concerned it owes much to Garvey, specifically to his preaching about the God of Ethiopia, his Back-to-Africa imperative, and, less directly, to a millenial 'prophecy' attributed to him which told black people to 'Look to Africa when a black king shall be crowned for the day of deliverance is near'. [29]

4
Babylon:
The Rise and Development
of the Rastafarian Movement
in Jamaica and Britain

Roll King Alfa, Roll King David, Roll
with Babylon away.
Come to give the wicked payment of
Great Babylon Reward.

Rasta song

Before leaving for England in 1935, Garvey is believed to have predicted the imminent redemption of Africa, telling his followers: 'It is in the wind. It is coming. One day like a storm it will be here.'[1] Garvey, as we have seen, was not the first to inspire black Jamaicans with this type of millenarian dream, which led them to believe that very soon, and as a race, they would witness the advent of a new dispensation and experience the total transformation here on this earth of their existence. Alexander Bedwell, the Jamaican preacher, had often proclaimed the imminent end of what he saw as white rule and exploitation of black people in Jamaica, whilst James Morris Webb, in an article, 'A Black Man Will be the Coming Universal King', published in 1919, spoke the same kind of salvationist message.[2] And in *The Black Man's Bible,* compiled during the First World War by Robert Athlyi Rogers, there is a chapter devoted to the black man's destiny after the final battle of the nations, Armageddon.

The millenial theme, then, was widespread in popular black Jamaican thought by the time Garvey departed from London. Furthermore, other black Jamaicans, familiar with the writings and proclamations of some of those already mentioned, began in the 1930s to preach that the redemption of the black race was close at hand. Prominent among these were Leonard P. Howell, who was acquainted with *The Black Man's Bible,* Robert Hinds, once a follower of Bedward, and two members of the Egyptian Secret Masonic Order, H. Archibald Dunkley and Nathaniel Hibbert. There was also the Garveyite

Ferdinand Ricketts and perhaps the most politically minded of them all, Paul Earlington, who was to establish a Jamaican branch of the Ethiopian World Federation.

Howell, Hibbert, Dunkley, and Hinds, all clergymen, claimed to be recipients of the revelation that the crowning of Ras Tafari as Emperor of Ethiopia in 1930 was a clear sign that the Scriptures were about to be fulfilled. Ras Tafari (better known to most people as Haile Selassie) was, they believed, the black messiah foretold in the Scriptures (Revelation 5: 2-5; 19: 16; Daniel 7: 3; Psalm 68: 31) who would lead the black race out of its captivity in Babylon (white-dominated society) and back to the African continent, the land without evil.

To these men and others, Ras Tafari was the 'God of Ethiopia' about whom Garvey had preached, the black king whom he prophesied would be crowned in Africa as the day of deliverance drew near. This message was taken in the early 1930s by Howell, Hibbert, Dunkley, and Archibald to the blacks, some of them Garveyites, of Kingston, capital of Jamaica, and from there it travelled slowly across the island. To all intents and purposes this was the beginning of the Rastafarian movement, a movement that proclaimed the divinity of Ras Tafari and looked to him to destroy white domination and restore to the black race, God's 'favoured race' and a superior race, its destiny, dignity, pride, and status of which it had been deprived by enslavement and colonialism.

Howell's preaching attracted attention from ordinary people and government alike. Everywhere he went he proclaimed the divinity of Haile Selassie and announced that the Emperor of Ethiopia and not George V of England was the king and ruler of the black people. He insisted, further, on the duty incumbent on black people to prepare to return to Africa. He distributed a Rasta bible, much of the content of which was derived from *The Black Man's Bible,* wherein it was stated that the authentic version of the Bible, written in Amharic, had been distorted by white people who had turned God and his prophets into white men.

In his Rasta bible and preaching Howell presented Haile Selassie as the returned messiah and his coming as a clear sign that the black race, as descendants of the people of the Torah, would soon return to Africa and once there would regain its position and status for so long denied it by the whites. He also emphasized, and this has become an important tenet of the Rastafarian movement, that God and/or the divine is present in the innermost reaches of every man. Howell was arrested along with Hinds in 1934 and sentenced to two years in prison for sedition. After his release he established the Ethiopian Salvation Society, centred on Pinnacle commune in the hills outside Kingston;

it was there that the practice of smoking ganja (marijuana) was introduced which has since become the principal ritual of the Rastafarian movement.

Meanwhile the Italian invasion of Ethiopia in 1936 had focused the world's attention on that country and its emperor. The invasion dealt a terrible blow to African pride, hopes, and aspirations, and summoned up previously untapped reserves of bitterness against what the black writer Ayadele Taylor scornfully referred to as 'the great civilization of the white race'.[3] Taylor added: 'A "civilized" nation condemned Ethiopia . . . Surely Christ must have wept to see those tortuous instruments sent across the sea, instruments that surely were the creation of some demon brain in a careless nation . . . and they linked his [Christ's] name with this enterprise.'[4]

The Italian invasion not only gave rise to anger and scorn but also to a greater interest in and commitment to Ethiopia, symbol of Africa's self-pride and courage, and to the Ethiopian cause. To quote Taylor again: 'But to Africa you [Ethiopia] have given much, you are a great example to our simple race, of a sincere and courageous if not a perfect race. Africans, oppressed but undefeated nation, arouse your children for a new civilization.'[5]

The Italians were driven out of Ethiopia in 1941 and Haile Selassie was given much of the credit for this by both Africans and the British. The Rastafarians interpreted Haile Selassie's return to Ethiopia as the fulfilment of the book of Revelation 19: 11-19 concerning the first battle of the End, in which the King of kings and Lord of lords deals mortal ruin to his enemies and destroys Babylon. The British, for their part, in broadcasts and war propaganda materials distributed in the colonies, presented Haile Selassie as a 'great African' and the 'model Emperor of Abyssinia [Ethiopia]', who had not only done much to defeat the Italians but who was also engaged in establishing a 'New Order'.[6]

The creation by Haile Selassie in 1937 of the Ethiopian World Federation (E.W.F.), a branch of which was opened in Jamaica by Paul Earlington in 1938, also gave considerable impetus to the Rastafarian movement. The E.W.F.'s main aims were to unify black people throughout the world for the purpose of defending the integrity of Ethiopia, which by divine right belonged to all black people, and the regaining by all African states of their independence.

It was not until the 1950s, however, that the Rastafarian movement began to grow rapidly in Jamaica and from there to spread to other parts of the Caribbean, the United States, and Britain. In the main this millenarian movement had appealed to the lower classes, the poor and disaffected black Jamaicans. It gave them the firm hope of a better, indeed a totally different life in the here and now in Africa, under

Haile Selassie (*Topham*)

a divine ruler who was one of their race. It also provided the ideology, institutions, and the rituals by means of which this hope could be sustained, and denounced the enemy — the white ruling élite and all those black Jamaicans, whether in government, business or the law enforcement agencies, who associated with them.

The police and the law enforcement agencies in general became a special object of hatred as members began to be jailed in increasing numbers for ganja (marijuana) offences and, in particular members of the Nyabingi section of the movement, for resorting to violence as a means of resolving the problems of poverty and discrimination. This approach, however, ran counter to the more generally accepted belief that deliverance from these 'evils' would come not as a result of human effort but through divine intervention. It is this belief that distinguishes the mainstream of the Rastafarian movement from the Garveyites, who placed greater emphasis on the need to search for a human rather than a supernatural solution to the problems of black people. For Garveyites the stress was on self-reliance; for the Rastafarian it was on divine intervention in the person of the messiah, Haile Selassie.

Two important developments occurred in 1955, both of which strengthened the belief that the black race was about to be saved through the divine intervention of Haile Selassie. First of all a member of the Ethiopian World Federation (E.W.F.) from New York brought Jamaicans a message from Ethiopia informing them that Haile Selassie was building a Navy and that ships would sail to American and possibly Jamaican ports.[7] This was taken to mean that the Emperor was preparing to repatriate blacks to their homeland. Secondly, the E.W.F. told its branches in Jamaica later in the same year that Haile Selassie had decided to set aside land for the black people of the West to cultivate on their return to Ethiopia. All of this created an atmosphere of great excitement and expectancy; many wanted to be repatriated immediately, and in 1956 some were seen at the port in Kingston awaiting the arrival of a ship which would transport them to Ethiopia.

It is, of course, extremely difficult to generalize about Rastafarians and their beliefs, for this is not a church movement with hierarchical structures, highly developed institutions, and a systematic theology. As one study graphically puts it: 'there is no Rasta Church. There are the odd backyard cells with an outhouse daubed in Ethiopian red, green and gold, a few big crude maps and diagrams on the fence showing the distribution of the races in the world and a few yellowed snapshots of Selassie . . . there is no priesthood, no clergy, no ceremonial. There isn't even a consensus of belief.'[8] It is *personal experience,* as much as anything else, which determines the validity or otherwise of a statement, truth, or belief.

Thus while some Rastafarians have held to the belief that the existing social, political, and economic order will be totally transformed through divine intervention, others have sought to change society radically by the use of political and other, human or natural, means. As it expanded and assumed a more political character in the second half of the 1950s and the 1960s, the Rastafarian movement began to attract far more attention from the authorities, and in 1957 there was a fierce backlash against the movement after the killing of a woman in Kingston, allegedly by a Rastafarian.

Extremely critical of the established churches, as well as of the government, the bureaucracy, the professional classes, and the police, the Rastafarians came to be seen as a serious threat to all existing forms of authority. These were scornfully dismissed by Rastafarians as mere instruments of Babylon, a system of total oppression and exploitation, created by whites and which certain blacks even helped to perpetuate. It is not always easy to assess the relative significance of race and class in Rastafarian thinking, and in the concrete situation it is sometimes impossible to differentiate between the two. Fanon's words perhaps best express their view of existing socio-economic relationships in Babylon: 'You are rich because you are white and you are white because you are rich.'[9]

March 1958 witnessed the first Rastafarian Universal Convention held at the movement's headquarters, Back-o-Wall, Kingston, Jamaica, and here the more militant members provoked consternation and dismay when they attempted unsuccessfully to capture the city in the name of Haile Selassie. A similar incident happened in Spanish Town later in the same year and at this point, confused and alarmed, members of the middle class and the academic world called for an in-depth inquiry into the beliefs, aims, and aspirations of the movement.

The government was later to commission an inquiry[10] but this did nothing to pacify the more militant members of the movement or dampen the enthusiasm of those who sought repatriation. In fact in 1959 thousands of black Jamaicans, including many Rastafarians, sold all they had to obtain a ticket for a passage to Ethiopia from Claudius Henry, a self-proclaimed prophet and founder of the African Reform Church. They were to be disappointed and dispossessed: after waiting on the pier at Kingston, once again no ship arrived.

Henry was charged with fraud and bound over to keep the peace on this occasion, and in 1960 sentenced to six years in prison for conspiring with others to overthrow the government. Later in the same year his son Ronald was charged, along with eight others, with murder and hanged in March 1961. The militancy, however, continued, and confrontation after confrontation ensued between groups of Rastas and the police, until the government reached the conclusion that the ganja weed (not used by all Rastafarians) was to a large extent the cause of the violence. Attempts were made to stamp out this practice, but to no avail.

During the 1960s the movement developed into an even more complex phenomenon, appealing as it did not only to the unemployed and the poor but also to some of the more privileged groups, students in particular. This, to some extent, resulted in the development of a somewhat different theory of repatriation. While some continued to cling tenaciously to the belief that salvation could only be achieved by physical repatriation to Africa, for others repatriation was to be understood symbolically: it meant above all else a return to Africa at the level of consciousness. It involved mental decolonization, a process of deconversion, of turning away from the ethos, mores, and values of colonial society and a reconversion to the African view and way of life. Educated and brought up to appreciate and admire the history and achievements of Europeans, they were now suffering, so to speak, from loss of memory and were therefore without any authentic reason, feeling, or coherence. For these people repatriation consisted of erasing one interpretation, philosophy, and way of life — the Babylonian one — and restoring another — the African and/or Ethiopian one. However, these differences of emphasis and interpretation apart, what the Rastafarian movement continued to offer all Rastas was the promise of redemption.

The high point for many Rastafarians was the state visit to Jamaica in late August 1966 by Haile Selassie, King of kings, conquering Lion of the Tribes of Judah. People from every part of the island assembled at the airport in Kingston to greet the Emperor, and when the royal plane with the lion painted on the side was spotted there was such frenzy and disorder that Selassie was obliged to wait for over an hour before he could leave the aircraft. It is worth noting that neither on this occasion nor at any other time did Haile Selassie either acknowledge or deny his divinity. But this made little difference, for whether he approved or not he had divinity thrust upon him by his followers, who believed he was their God and worshipped him as such.

It was during this visit to Jamaica, some observers believe, that the Emperor advised his followers to strive first of all for liberation in Jamaica before turning to Africa.[11] If this advice was given it made little difference to many, especially the older members, who continued to believe that physical repatriation was a necessary condition for redemption. Some of the new recruits, as we have seen, among them musicians and university students, saw the pathway to salvation lying more in the direction of a greater self-awareness and consciousness of their African identity than in the actual, physical return to Africa.

With this shift in interpretation of 'doctrine' the Rastafarian movement took on a more active political role in Jamaica, developing and expressing a radical critique not only of plantation and colonial society but also of neo-colonial Jamaican society. Meanwhile reggae artists like Bob Marley and the Wailers were on their way to producing 'sounds of reality' — the pent-up, often inarticulated feelings, anxieties, frustrations, and sufferings of the oppressed, apocalytic sounds of a society in the throes of radical transformation.

One of the most radical critiques of colonial and neo-colonial society came from the pen of the Guyanese specialist in West African history Dr Walter Rodney, banned from the University of the West Indies in 1968 and later assassinated in Guyana. In his pamphlet *Groundings* (a term used to describe Rastafarian 'reasoning sessions' and/or meetings), which comprises six lectures delivered in Jamaica in 1968 and for which the author was branded a subversive by the government, Rodney discusses the Jamaican situation in terms of slavery and the colonial heritage. He considers the relevance of black power and revolutionary ideology and suggests that the main aim of the movement, and of all black movements, should be to break with imperialism, to promote the assumption of power by the black masses, and to undertake the cultural reconstruction of society in the image of blacks. Rodney did not want to see blacks in power in present society, but in a radically changed society. His lectures gave a new impetus to radical forces in Jamaica and the Caribbean. [12]

But it was the musicians rather than the intellectuals who appear to have exerted the greater influence on Jamaican politics, at least in the short term. By the early 1970s the Rastafarians had emerged as an important factor in Jamaican politics and politicians like Michael Manley, leader of the People's National Party (P.N.P.) and prime minister from 1972–80, came to depend heavily on Marley and other influential Rastafarians for support. In the opinion of some observers, Bob Marley was the 'power in the land', and with his endorsement Manley won a landslide victory in the Jamaican elections in 1976. [13] Marley, further, was also becoming a 'power' outside Jamaica, among young blacks, and others, in Britain and the United States as he 'preached' the end of Babylon and the need for a 'new consciousness'.

Meanwhile, Haile Selassie, toppled by the military in September 1974, died while under house arrest in Ethiopia in August 1975. Many Rastafarians refused to accept that their messiah was dead and reports to the contrary were dismissed as part of the Babylonian conspiracy which, through false propaganda, was trying to strike at the very heart of the movement. At first sight this appears like a refusal on the part of the Rastafarians to acknowledge and accept the facts. However, to them talk of the death of Haile Selassie was irrational: only those imbued with the colonial mentality would use the term 'death' to describe the condition of a person after the heart stops beating. Real life is much more than living in the body, and what is more, Rastafarians 'knew' their God was alive for they continued to experience his vital, living presence and were totally convinced that, in the words of one of their lyrics,

> As Jah [God/King] was in the beginning
> Jah is now and ever mus' be . . .[14]

The spread of the Rastafarian movement to Britain. The movement spread to other islands in the Caribbean, and also to Africa, Australia and New Zealand, Canada, the United States and Europe, in particular Britain. It first appeared in Britain in the mid-1950s with the attempt to organize a Rastafarian United Afro-West Indian Brotherhood in 1955. Today there are two main branches of the movement in Britain, one calling itself the Twelve Tribes of Israel, to which Bob Marley belonged, the other being known as the Ethiopian Orthodox Church, which forbids its members to wear dreadlocks and, more significantly, refuses to acknowledge the divinity of Haile Selassie.

While there are a small number of white Rastafarians, the vast majority of the movement's adherents are from black working-class families living in London and other cities. Possessing little appeal for over a decade or more, the movement began to attract an increasing number of young black people, most of them under twenty-five, from the late 1960s, giving rise to consternation and alarm among teachers, parents, and others. Many of the new recruits to the Rastafarian movement were, like their parents, members of the West Indian Pentecostal Congregations in Britain that were affiliated to one or other of the three major West Indian Pentecostalist churches: the New Testament Church of God, the Church of God of Prophecy, and the Apostolic Church of Jesus Christ. These churches, which have basically the same beliefs as other Pentecostalists churches in Britain, encourage greater spontaneity, enthusiasm, and participation by the laity and it was for this purpose, among others, that they were established.[15] They also served to cushion many West Indians against the harsh realities of life in Britain, against the alienation, discrimination, and racialism that they felt they experienced in everyday life. Furthermore, these churches, some West Indians maintain, also owe their existence to the fact that the 'English' churches did not appear to welcome them in their congregations. There was the added reason that a large proportion of the 260,000 West Indian immigrants who came' to Britain between 1955-62 was genuinely concerned at what it saw as the lack of enthusiasm for religion in this country and fearing that there would be a turning away from religion on a large scale involved itself in establishing new and 'relevant' churches.

From Pentecostalists to the Rastafarians. What was regarded as 'relevant' by immigrants in the 1950s and early 1960s increasingly came to be seen by many of their children as obsolete and purely a form of escapism. The Pentecostalist churches offered a limited number of their congregations a certain status and all of them the hope of a better life through the sudden intervention of Jesus Christ, who on his second coming would lift the yoke of oppression and give justice to the patient, meek, and humble of heart.[16] Their turn, in other words, would eventually come. There was no question of developing a new consciousness or awareness of self, or a totally different approach to life and set of values. What was being sought, it appeared, was a purely symbolic transformation of the social order. To the young this patient, even passive, response to the problems confronting themselves and their communities was bound to fail. Like Garvey they were moving towards the view that in white society whatever they did, however 'successful' they were, however much they conformed, they would never be regarded as equals.

The influence of 'Black Power'. Disenchanted with Pentecostalism, many young blacks became acquainted with movements such as Black Power, which offered a political solution to the problems facing black immigrants. At the same time, the Rastafarian movement had begun to adopt a more militant, political character, without losing its religious foundations.

The Black Power phenomenon was not entirely new, owing much to the activities and writings of black spokesmen of a previous era, among them Edward Blyden, Marcus Garvey, John Price Mars, Aimé Césaire, Henry Silvester Williams, George Padmore, C. L. James, and Franz Fanon. In the 1960s the movement was strongest in the United States and had developed an ideology that was flexible enough to permit the term 'black' to be applied to all those who were oppressed throughout the Third World. As one spokesman of the movement stated: 'We stretch our hands across the sea to the new independent states of India. We hail the Indonesians in their struggle for liberty. We are one with Africans in their effort to throw off the yoke of colonialism . . . The race problem has assumed worldwide proportions.'[17]

Others, like Stokely Carmichael, provided a somewhat narrower definition of the term black, while at the same time linking the Black Power movement to other radical movements in the Third World. While claiming that 'We got brothers in Africa, we got brothers in Cuba, we got brothers in India, we got brothers in Latin America, we got brothers all over the world', Carmichael nevertheless insisted that black people throughout the world must recognize Africa as their homeland and join together to defeat western imperialism. [18]

A crucial element in this struggle against imperialism was the development of a black ideology of cultural difference, something that appealed to Rastafarians and which was in itself a response to a European tendency to present black people as curiosities possessing strange characteristics. For example, Rousseau popularized the idea, brought back from Tahiti by Bourgainville and accepted as part of psychiatric theory until quite recently, that black people living in a state of primitive simplicity never became insane. [19] But the idea that a 'primitive' was incapable of mental illness was developed over time and came to mean that in a sense he was already disturbed in this way. The African, as Kipling viewed him, was 'half-devil-half-child'; madness was his normal condition. [20]

Towards self-definition.   Defined negatively and pejoratively by others for so long, the Black Power, Black Muslim, Black Jewish, and Rastafarian movements made it an integral part of their overall objective of black emancipation to establish the right to self-definition, which would involve amongst other things establishing the field of confrontation, determing the order of priorities and the issues to be discussed and negotiated, and — by no means the least important part of the strategy — deciding the meaning of 'words'. On this last point Stokely Carmichael quoted *Through the Looking-Glass:* ' "When I use a word", Humpty Dumpty said in a rather scornful tone, "It means just what I choose it to mean, neither more nor less." "The question is ", said Alice, "whether you can make words mean so many different things." "The question is", said Humpty Dumpty, "which is to be master — that's all." ' [21]

Thus while Pentecostalism, and even more so mainstream Christianity, came to be seen by greater numbers of young black people in Britain as a form of passive acceptance of the status quo, of white society's values and definition of black people, the more aggressive, political, even at times militant approach of the Rastafarian movement, influenced by Black Power and similar movements, began to attract their attention and in the 1970s it came to fill the vacuum left when Black Power went into decline with the death of its leaders, among them George Jackson, Malcolm X, and Michael X.

Jamaican Rasta wearing a 'tam' (*J. Allan Cash Photolibrary*)

Through the way they dress, their dreadlocks, their 'tams' (headgear) in the Ethiopian colours of red, black, green, and gold, their music and general lifestyle, and their way of 'living naturally', the Rastafarians assert their right to define themselves, to decide who they were, and who they are, to determine how they should live and the values they should pursue. Everywhere among the new generation of black youth in Britain in the late 1960s and the 1970s one can detect this more aggressive, self-assertive manner. For example at the Black Youth conference of May 1971 a spokesman told his enthusiastic audience that as black people they should 'decide through their own experiences . . . damn well assert themselves . . . bring to a halt London transport', and that 'without militancy we can expect nothing'. [22] The general view now was that black people had been too passive, too resigned, too conformist.

The Rastafarian movement, then, was influenced by and influenced this development of a more assertive, political response among black youth in Britain. Black musicians weaved into their songs Rastafarian themes such as the destruction of Babylon, and many blacks, though not members of the movements, wore dreadlocks, dressed and walked Rastafarian style and used Rastafarian language in an endeavour to raise their consciousness of themselves as Africans and by way of shocking society into realizing that they were no longer prepared to turn themselves into deluded hybrids by conforming to the host society's standards, only to discover that they were still regarded as aliens and a threat to the general well-being.

Rising status and recognition. The Rastafarians, as they intended, sent shock waves through British society and aroused opposition from both black and white people. While some hoped this was simply a passing phase and closed their eyes to it, others saw looming on the horizon an intractable racial and social problem. The churches for their part began slowly in the mid-1970s to build bridges with the young Rastafarians in an effort to diffuse some of the bitterness that existed between them — by, for example, offering the local church hall for their services. And by 1982 the Roman Catholic Church's Commission for Racial Justice had produced a report in which it recognized 'Rastafarianism' as a 'valid religion' and advocated dialogue 'with a view to mutual learning and sharing'. [23] Furthermore, clergymen of other churches were taking the Home Office to task for allegedly dismissing the movement as 'just another youth cult'. According to one Unitarian cleric, Rastafarians were 'a distinct religious movement, linked to the Judaeo-Christian tradition, but distinguished by the special place offered to the figure of Haile Selassie, as an affirmation that the divine indwelling is as true for black people as for any others'. [24]

Whatever its thoughts on these interpretations of the movement's 'theology', by the end of 1981 even the Home Office was prepared to make concessions to Rastafarians on religious grounds. In 1976, in a circular containing guidelines to prisons, the Home Office was reported to have stated that Rastafarians should be treated as members of a cult in the same way as skinheads or hippies. But following the Scarman Inquiry into the Brixton disorders, which stated that 'The Rastafarians, their faith and their aspirations, deserve more understanding and more sympathy than they get from the British people', [25] it decided to change the prison rules in respect of Rastafarians. For example, where it existed, the practice of cutting Rastafarians' dreadlocks was to cease. However the ganja smoking ritual, not necessarily adhered to by all Rastafarians, and the concept of Babylon were probably the two main reasons why the Home Office did not give formal religious status to the movement. The Rastafarian movement is but one of a number of 'new religions' to give rise to the thorny issue of whether or not an exemption from existing legislation should be allowed for certain kinds of what are claimed to be religiously motivated actions, in this case the smoking of ganja. Decision-making in this area is an extremely delicate matter and in principle involves a genuine concern for granting the fullest expression of religious freedom consistent with established norms, secular regulations, and public order.

In the not too distant past even some of the established Christian churches encountered this problem — for example during the Prohibition in the United States, when legislation had to be introduced to allow the use of sacramental wine. [25] The ritual of peyote-chewing engaged in by American Indians was legalized by the Californian Supreme Court in 1964 on the grounds that to prohibit its use would be to strike at the 'theological heart' of the sect (since 1918 the Native American Church) and place a burden on the free exercise of religion. Other states, Arizona, Montana, New Mexico among them, have amended their narcotics laws to allow an exemption for the ritual use of peyote by Indians. [26] The exemption in this case, however, is something of an exception. Other appeals in the United States for exemption from narcotics laws have not been upheld. Many groups using psychedelic drugs to generate religious experience, and known as the 'psychedelic churches', sought exemption without success, while others, such as the Church of the Awakening, failed to obtain exemption for the use of drugs including peyote, for religious and therapeutic purposes. [27]

With its rise in status and 'respectability', the call for a deeper and more objective understanding of the movement by Lord Scarman, who makes the point that from the Rastafarian viewpoint the use of ganja is not necessarily any more dangerous than the use of alcohol, [28] and the decision of mainstream churches publicly to pronounce the movement a 'genuine' religion, it seems likely that the use of ganja by Rastafarians will over time cease to be a reason, as it has been in the past, for dismissing out of hand both its views of the world and the real purposes for which it exists.

Some Rastafarians have welcomed the status and recognition accorded them and even accept now that it is perfectly possible for them to work within the structures of Babylon as 'a normal member of society', although the basic aim of the movement remains repatriation to Africa. [29] Others have rejoined one or other of the Pentecostalist or established churches, some have become Muslims, while others have simply dropped out of the movement and 'religion' altogether. Some of those who have rejoined one or other of the churches have done so largely from disillusionment. Having once accepted that being a Rasta would change everything in their life they came to see, as one ex-member who was with the movement for five years expressed it, that 'there is no point in attempting to radically change the world; there is only room for a little improvement in this life, and the main thing is to save one's soul and this can be done'. [30]

Among those who have left the movement some have done so because, they say, 'it has been made into a religion and now has all the faults of other religions', [31] while others have left convinced that the movement 'cannot work in a materialistic society like Britain'. [32] In Jamaica or Africa, they explain, the movement makes sense, for there people, with their own plots of land, can live 'naturally' and help one another; but this 'natural' way is impossible in a highly industrialized, materialistic society like Britain. Then there are ex-members who claim that they are now fully conscious of who they are, are aware of 'the structural oppression of white society', and who therefore no longer feel any need for the movement. Further, they would like to explode the myth concerning the divinity of Haile Selassie, whom they have come to regard as an oppressor and exploiter of his people. [33] A number of others have become Muslims, believing that Islam, in its teaching about women and in other respects, is closer than any other religion to the African way of life. [34]

The death of Bob Marley in 1981 created a number of problems for the movement. Although in no formal sense its leader, Marley generated considerable enthusiasm for all things Rastafarian, and though its message cannot be reduced to reggae, albums such as *Rastaman Vibration* perhaps did more than anything else to spread

Bob Marley (*J. Allan Cash Photolibrary*)

that message and arouse interest in a movement that has no organized system of recruitment and where for the most part the diffusion of its beliefs has been through individual contact.

To see decline from 1981 onwards as the natural state of the movement seems a little premature. While there are no reliable statistics that would enable an accurate estimate to be made of the number of adherents in 1981, there are probably fewer members now than there were then. Be this as it may, the evidence suggests that there exists a solid core of deeply convinced and committed Rastas who are engaged in learning Amharic, accept the movement's dietary regulations (for example the avoidance of food, with the exception of fruit, from unknown sources), and who are as convinced as ever that redemption awaits them in Africa. [35] According to informants, although the numbers remain small, more members are now returning to Africa than previously.

One of the largest Rastafarian groups in Africa is in Accra, capital of Ghana in West Africa. One of the pioneers of this Rasta commune with its headquarters, a three-roomed wooden house situated amid the embassies and sumptuous multi-storeyed houses in an affluent suburb of the capital, is the Jamaican Wolde Mikal. After leaving Jamaica in the early 1970s Mikal spent some time in London working among the youth in Brixton before 'returning' to Africa (Ghana) in 1974. While others simply talked about returning to Africa, Mikal took action, believing he had to return because 'according to prophecy sooner or later the children have to come home'. [36] Allocated two 50-acre plots by local chiefs, he and his 'brothers' produce their own food and spend a considerable amount of time 'educating' the local people about the movement. Mikal advises those Rastas remaining in Britain to leave 'Babylon' while the gate to Africa is still open, and promises them that when they reach paradise they will never want to return to Babylon. Another commune of Rastas, mainly Ghanaian and about 200 strong, is to be found at Kongo in Labadi on the coast. [37]

As for those who bide their time in Babylon, they appear to be of two types: one very exclusivist and critical of white society, even opposing the idea of allowing whites to become members of the movement, and the other less hostile in its criticism of the established churches and the wider society as a whole and open to contact with all groups in the search for solutions to social and other problems. For this last mentioned group the biggest attraction of the Rastafarian movement lies in the feeling they experience of being wanted, and the freedom and opportunity it provides for helping their own people in particular, but others also, to survive in today's society. Rastas in this group tend to be open and ecumenical; as one informant explained, they are 'against separating people in one way and another' and 'want to help and co-operate with others who assist those who are down and out'.[38]

There is evidence to suggest that the Rastafarian movement, and other African religions, have enabled members to survive in contemporary society; paradoxically, it is possible that the movement may in the long term prove to be a force for integration rather than division and segregation. In New Zealand, Rastafarian influence contributed, according to some observers, to the integration into the wider society of a number of disaffected Maori youth.[39] And in Britain there are black people, some Rastafarians, others not, who feel that the movement has helped them, as some Ethiopian informants have ironically stated, 'to understand who they are, to be proud of themselves, and to feel more at ease and less threatened by the wider society'.[40]

All of this is not to suggest that Rastafarians have gone soft on white society; their relations with Babylon on the whole, and in particular with the police, remain poor. The ostentatious rejection of white, especially middle-class values, persists, as does the dramatic juxtaposing of black and white in the fields of history, economics, religion, and politics. Unlike Pentecostalist churches and others which they believe share the symbolic system of white society, Rastafarians for whom God is black see salvation as lying in adherence to a black system of values, way of life, and interpretation of reality.

Whatever their symbolic system may share with Babylon, it is nevertheless the case that the fortunes of the Pentecostalist and Holiness churches with a predominantly black membership compare very favourably with those of the Rastafarian movement. These churches are expanding as rapidly today, and perhaps even more rapidly, than at any time during the past decade, with a growth of around 6 per cent a year. In fact, along with the independent evangelical churches and the House Church movement, these 'black' churches are the only churches in contemporary Britain to show a sustained increase in membership in recent years.

To some black people, among them Rastafarians, these black churches are a bastion of reaction in the black community cherished by a generation that has failed to come to terms with political necessities; to others they are the guardians of a tradition of Caribbean religiosity and an appropriate cultural and political response to the situation of blacks in Britain, who unlike the Rastafarians refuse to indulge in millenarian fantasy and rhetoric and have decided, realistically, that they belong where they are.

5
Beliefs

*Jah lives! . . . If you want to know where I
head rest, I head rest with Jah.*

Bob Marley

Something has already been said in previous chapters about
Rastafarian beliefs and here we propose to consider these in a more
systematic way. However it should be made clear from the outset that
the Rastafarian movement has no agreed system of beliefs, no agreed
credo equivalent to the Nicene Creed, the Thirty Nine Articles, or
the five main articles of Islam (see Qur'an 2: 177). As we shall see below,
attempts have been made to summarize Rastafarian beliefs but these
have never been granted the status of a catechism.

Nevertheless, it would be misleading to suggest that Rastafarians
are without a theology. They spend a great deal of time reflecting on
the Bible and 'reasoning' about ideas of a universal nature and about
the ultimate objects of human enquiry: the nature of God, of man,
of the world and the relationship between them, the meaning of life,
providence and destiny.

Discovering truth. In the Rastafarian movement no one member
or group has the authority to lay down what the rest should believe
or to decide what is orthodox and what is heterodox. Nor can this be
easily decided on the basis of practice, for attendance and participation
in worship and ritual are not obligatory.

Rastafarians must 'test' what they hear and read, discerning truth
by intuitive understanding and experience. This can be done by
communicating or 'head resting' with Jah (God) on an individual basis
and also collectively at 'reasoning' sessions and/or 'groundings', where
members develop and articulate an understanding of themselves and
the world derived from reflection on the Bible and their own history

and experience as individuals and as a people.

Truth, then, is grounded in a particular kind of experience known as 'dread', which has been defined as 'the confrontation of a people with a primordial but historically denied racial selfhood'.[1] It is also 'inspired' and authenticated by an external, objective source, the Bible, when correctly understood and interpreted. In what they consider to be its original authentic form, the Bible provides an objective account of the early history of the black race and of their 'identity' and destiny as a favoured race, the people of God. However, the Bible in translation — it was, the Rastafarians claim, originally written in stone in Amharic — cannot be taken literally. The translators, ignorant of Amharic, mistranslated some sections and in order to conceal from black people their real history and identity purposely omitted others. Through meditation, which puts them in communion with Jah, and through experience and intuitive knowledge Rastafarians come to realize what is true and what is false in the Bible, and the extent and meaning of the sections omitted, and thereby arrive at a rounded, faithful rendering of its contents.

Approached critically in this way the Bible can be used to interpret the past and present and to predict the future. But what it teaches can never be divorced from what is learnt from the 'book within', from intuition and experience, which come from the inner divine presence. If these two sources of inspiration and truth do not go hand in hand then, the Rastafarians believe, the 'external' or 'objective' source, the Bible, could be used once again, as was the case in the past, as an instrument for oppression and enslavement rather than a means of self-discovery and liberation.

The internalization of authority. From what has just been said it is clear that ultimately the most valid criterion for establishing truth is personal experience. Rastafarians do not wish to be led by others, but prefer to listen to and be guided by Jah. They remain sceptical about everything they hear and read until they 'test' or discern its truth by intuitive religious experience, which is the principal means of validating truth. The principle of experience as the authority for truth, taken alongside that of individual exegesis, makes it impossible for the movement to be dogmatic in the presentation of its beliefs, and explains why it can be quite appropriately described as 'creedless'. In fact the conviction held by many Rastafarians that the group has no dogma is so strong that it has itself become something of a dogma. Of course the knowledge that Jah dwells within provides the rationale for this individual autonomy and ability to discover truth.

Knowledge/faith. From experience and a correct reading of the

Bible, which substantiates what is learnt from experience, the Rastafarian can claim to possess true knowledge about God, man, and the purpose of history, as distinct from the 'mere' faith which Christians, for example, receive.

The Rasta does not 'simply' believe in; he 'knows' Jah and his purposes for man. Knowing Jah is ultimately a matter of knowing oneself, of realizing that the inner self is divine. This is not only a way of realizing one's potential, of enhancing respect for the self, but also of shielding it against doubt, ambiguity, and even anomy.

'Mere' belief, then, is not something that appeals to Rastafarians for their religious quest consists in 'knowing' with certainty who they are and where they are going, in determining events rather than being determined by them, in exchanging the mentality and status of slave imposed upon them by Babylon for that of master. By 'knowing' is not meant, of course, the rational approach to understanding of the philosopher, but something more akin to the biblical meaning of the term as found in such injunctions as 'Be still and know that I am God'.

Central 'truths'.   Granted its in-built mechanism for revision and development, its approach to discerning truth, and its emphasis on personal experience as the ultimate criterion of truth, observers have nonetheless attempted, and not altogether unreasonably, to identify the central 'truths' and/or ideas of the Rastafarian movement. In the 1950s, according to one social scientist, a nucleus of six central ideas were shared by almost all members of the movement. These were: (1) black people are descendants and/or reincarnations of the early Israelites and were exiled for their transgressions; (2) Haile Selassie is the living God; (3) paradise and/or the promised land is Ethiopia and/or Africa, whilst Babylon is hell; (4) black people are superior to whites; (5) black people will soon take their revenge on whites and compel the latter to serve them; (6) their God (Jah) and Emperor will arrange for their repatriation to Ethiopia.[2]

By 1960 scholars were suggesting that the central teachings could be reduced to four: (1) Rastafari (Haile Selassie) is the living God; (2) Ethiopia is the home of the black person; (3) redemption, which will soon occur, is by repatriation; (4) the ways of white people are evil.[3] Shortly afterwards another observer maintained that there were only *two* essential truths: (1) Ras Tafari is the living God; (2) salvation for black people is through repatriation to Africa.[4]

While these neat and tidy formulations of Rastafarian 'doctrines' have their use in pinpointing what over time would appear to have been central 'truths', it is important to keep in mind that there is neither one single nor several tenets which are strictly adhered to by all Rastas.

The situation is, and has been, that there are a number of complementary and often paradoxical truths advanced by way of explanation of the past, present, and future circumstances of black people. Here we can turn to a consideration of these truths.

Jah: the God within.   In many new religions today, especially those of Indian provenance such as the Divine Light Mission, Ishvara, and the Rajneesh Foundation, the emphasis is on realizing one's *own* divinity, on becoming God rather than simply believing in or even knowing God. As the founder of the Rajneesh movement, Bhagwan (God) Shree Rajneesh tells his followers: 'the real is to become God not to know God'; or as Mahesh Yogi, leader of Transcendental Meditation expresses it, 'The inner man is Divine, is fully Divine', and in the words of the Ishvara movement, 'Man is the only God'. [5]

While it certainly differs in many other respects from these Indian-oriented new religions, the Rastafarian movement places the same emphasis on the divine inner nature of man. There is no belief in a God out there, an unreachable God who is totally other. The only way to discover the divine is to search within, to descend into the innermost recesses of one's being, for it is only there that God can be located.

Divinity, however, is more recognizable in some individuals than in others, and most of all in Jah Rastafari, Haile Selassie (Power of the Trinity), whose immortal spirit dwells within all living things. This is a truth derived from individual and collective searching and corroborated by the Bible. As we have already seen, Rastafarians will point to the book of Revelation chapters 5 and 19 and the royal Psalms in support of the divinity of Haile Selassie.

Haile Selassie is given innumerable titles and cast in many roles. He is Almighty God (Jah), King of kings and Lord of lords, Conquering Lion of the tribe of Judah, Judge and Avenger, King Alpha and Queen Omega (thus male and female), Returned Messiah, Elect of God, and 'Elect of Himself'; at the same time he is a fellow traveller, a brother and/or a sister. And by way of consolidating their union with their God and realizing their own divinity some Rastas use a number of these titles and names of themselves, even referring to themselves as Jah Rastafari. [6]

For all Jah's apparent otherness, therefore, the divine is first and foremost to be sought within the individual.

The returned messiah.   Not unexpectedly, given its strong millenial strain, many of the titles applied to Haile Selassie refer to his messianic status. The Saviour of the World, the Mediator, the Christ, the Returned Messiah are some of the messianic titles frequently attributed to him.

The claim that he is the Returned Messiah is supported by reference to the fact that he is the King of kings and Lord of lords of Revelation 19, and further that he is, like Jesus, from the royal line of David. There is no incompatibility in the Rastafarian view between the messiahship of Jesus and that of Haile Selassie, for the former promised to come again and that second coming is realized to the full in the person of the latter.

Like other new religions, the Rastafarian movement gives an important place to Jesus in its thinking, but it also differs somewhat from other movements in its understanding of the life and mission of Jesus (see over for a synopsis of the conceptions of Jesus found in some new religions).

Rastafarians make a distinction between the Jesus that was preached to their ancestors during the era of slavery and the 'real' Jesus. The real Christ or Jesus of the Gospels was in their view black and more precisely a Rasta, a view which is supported by the movement's doctrine of reincarnation. Christ's mission was to redeem his people; he was the 'divine' saviour or messiah for the people of his time — an understanding of Christ's role also found in the Rajneesh Foundation and the Divine Light Mission, amongst other new religions.

After completing his mission Christ was not crucified, nor did he die in any other way; not unlike the hidden Imam of the Shi'a Muslims, he disappeared or went into another realm. The 'real' Jesus overcame death, continued to live on, and came again for the last time in the person of Haile Selassie. This Jesus, as distinct from the Jesus preached to the slaves, is a Jesus with whom Rastafarians, and indeed everyone, can identify and experience. The Jesus preached by whites, on the other hand, was a false god who served the interests and purposes of Babylon.

Now, however, the last days are at hand for the 'real' Jesus has made a decisive, definitive return in the person of Haile Selassie, who will give to all those who believe a share in his immortality. Furthermore, once alienated by the indoctrination they experienced at the hands of whites who preached to them about an unreal, dead Jesus, synonymous with the false gods of Babylon, the Rastafarians now have the opportunity to recover the memory, the awareness, the full consciousness of who they are, of their true humanity and destiny, by experiencing and participating in the divine life which they share with Jah Rastafari, who not only links them with their past but will also lead them to the promised land. But how is this salvation to be accomplished?

Sin and salvation. While almost all religions agree that suffering and injustice are not man's permanent condition, that there is a way out, they are not all in agreement about the nature of 'sin' or 'evil'

SOME NEW RELIGIONS AND THEIR CONCEPTIONS
OF JESUS AND HIS MISSION

(1) *Unification Church (Moonies)*
Jesus is not God himself, but the image of God through whom
the world was created. As the perfect man he is the model of the
universe, but not its creator. Jesus is saviour of the world in the
spiritual, but not in the physical sense. He did not complete his
mission because of the crucifixion and the fraud of John the
Baptist. The world awaits redemption in a physical sense.

(2) *Children of God/The Family of Love*
Jesus is God and Saviour. He is the bridegroom of the believers,
whose love may be experienced in a sexual manner.

(3) *Transcendental Meditation*
Jesus is God in that he realizes the divinity of man in a prototypical
way.
Jesus never suffered on the Cross, and had no need to atone
for man's sins.
Salvation consists in realizing one's higher self which is God.

(4) *Divine Light Mission*
The historical Jesus was the saviour of his time, Guru Maharaj Ji
of the present age.
The inner self is God and can only be experienced through the
meditation techniques devised by this movement.

(5) *Rajneesh Foundation*
Jesus was an enlightened master in the Buddhist sense. He had
no ego; he was amoral and contradicted himself in order to make
it impossible for his teaching to be built up into a dogmatic system.
He is also an avatar (reincarnation of Vishnu) in the Hindu
sense.
Bhagwan (God) Shree Rajneesh and Jesus possess the same
degree of Christ consciousness/enlightenment. Thus the former
has the authority to pass on the teachings of Jesus to the
contemporary world.
On the Cross Jesus became fully enlightened and spent the
remainder of his life in silence in Kashmir.

and what causes it, nor about how and when it will be overcome and salvation attained. All, of course, offer the means to conquer evil, some claiming that the path they offer is the only route to salvation.

Conceptions of salvation itself vary considerably from one religious tradition to another. Buddhism and Hinduism, for example, see it as the cessation of desire following on from *moksha,* liberation or release from *samsara*, the recurrent cycle of birth and rebirth. In other traditions, the Christian and Muslim being cases in point, salvation lies in unending bliss in God's paradise for true believers and torment without end for those who refuse to believe and follow the straight path. In Zoroastrianism salvation consists of the undreamt of, unprecedented intensification of human happiness and the incomprehensible joy derived from the vision of Ohramazd (Ahura Mazda). The wicked, on the other hand, are thrown into the deep abyss of hell, where they are punished according to their evil deeds.

Judaism is a messianic faith and one that holds that there will come a time of perfect peace when the fortunes of the Jewish people will be restored and all will be united in a common belief in God. This messianic age will unfold not in some distant, spiritual heaven or after-life but in the actual physical world in which we live, and the messiah who will inaugurate this reign of peace and justice will be a human, not a divine being, descended from the royal house of David.

The Rastafarian concept of salvation is perhaps closer to that of the Jewish faith than to any of the other religions outlined above. The Rastaman knows in his heart that salvation is a certainty. Moreover he knows that it has been foretold in the Bible. And while Babylon stands accused of the heinous crimes of slavery and exploitation which brought about the degradation and humiliation of black people, Rastafarians know that these crimes would never have been committed had the black race been faithful to Jah. Slavery, exile, and exploitation are thus seen as the punishment imposed upon their forefathers and which they have inherited for failure to live up to their calling as God's favoured people.

For the Rastafarian, moreover, exile in Babylon is the worst form of evil imaginable, the one which gives rise to the most intense suffering, and it is from this form of evil that they long to be saved. The path to salvation lies in the direction of Africa; it is only by returning there that the black person can be redeemed.

Some believe that this return is quite close at hand, that it will take place around the year 2000. Jah Rastafari, Haile Selassie, will then intervene to ensure their repatriation to Africa, variously understood as Ethiopia, anywhere in Africa, or anywhere African. In the meantime 'sufferation' must continue. However this is somewhat alleviated by 'good tunes' and the benefit some members claim to derive from the knowledge that they are already spiritually repatriated. Others prepare for the day of redemption by 're-educating' themselves in the African way and by striving for spiritual repatriation, which consists essentially in becoming fully aware of their African identity, in discovering the truth about themselves through 'head resting' with Jah.

Africa is the original Eden, the promised land, the 'land without Evil', a real heaven, which the righteous will inherit during an eternal age of justice, peace, freedom, and plenty. However, before the advent of this messianic age there has to be a day of judgement when the Babylonian political and economic system will be razed to the ground in apocalyptic fashion. Then Nature will reassert herself to take vengeance on all those who have flouted her laws, by denying them access to the promised land.

We have, then, in the Rastafarian movement a conception of salvation of the millenial type not unlike that found in Judaism and in a number of contemporary religions, among them the Unification Church (the Moonies), the Worldwide Church of God or Armstrongism, the Children of God or Family of Love, Lifewaves or Ishvara, the Rajneesh Foundation, and a majority of the Japanese new religions of the post-World War II era such as Sekai Kyussei Kyo (The Church of World Messianity) and Soka Gakkai (Value Creation Society). All or most of these movements are, or were at the outset, inspired by the hope of a salvation which is to be enjoyed by the elect or faithful as a group, in other words the concept of collective salvation. Salvation is further seen as imminent, in that it will come both soon and suddenly, as terrestrial, in the sense that it will be effected in this world and not in some spiritual, supernatural heaven, as involving a complete transformation of the present order, and therefore total, and as being accomplished primarily by supernatural means.

These are all characteristics of those movements referred to as premillenial, as distinct from the post-millenial types, which believe that the Second Advent will follow the establishment of the millenium and that it will be realized only very gradually and through the instrumentality of the elect. There is little or no room in the Rastafarian movement for this gradualist version of the millenium nor for the view that it will be accomplished by anything other than divine intervention.[7]

Millenialism: The salvation of the deprived?   A typical response to millenialism, especially of the premillenial kind, is to suggest that it is an expression of the utter hopelessness felt by the disinherited. There are several examples of millenial movements that have attracted the poor in the main, and to an extent this is true of the Rastafarian movement. On the other hand it is also the case that the wealthy and well-placed, the white and the black from the so-called developed and developing worlds, have joined religious movements of the premillenial type. In Britain today, and in North America, the majority of the members of new religions with a pronounced millenial dimension come from the middle classes, and there was also a distinct middle-class element in the millenial movements that emerged in Britain in the eighteenth and nineteenth centuries, whilst in North America millenialism has never been a product only of the poor.

There are numerous ways in which people can feel or believe themselves to be disadvantaged and deprived, and in the case of an individual or group some of these may overlap. Economic deprivation can be clearly determined in certain cases by objective criteria: it is possible, for example, to examine systematically whether in a particular society an individual or group can afford the necessities of life. This form of deprivation can also be a highly subjective matter when individuals or groups, who from an objective standpoint are relatively well-to-do, come to see themselves as economically deprived in relation to others who are even more well-to-do than themselves.

In addition to economic deprivation there is also social deprivation, which derives from a society's tendency to esteem certain ways of behaving, certain attributes and achievements, more than others and to award status, prestige, and opportunity for advancement accordingly. While the level of social status is usually determined by the social class to which an individual belongs, and which in turn is measured by economic criteria, the two do not always correspond exactly. Be that as it may, it is clear that in Britain today being unemployed, without educational qualifications, and black is going to mean not only relatively low social class but also relatively low social status.

Other forms of deprivation include ethical deprivation, where there exists a conflict between an individual's or group's values, ideals, and aspirations and those of the wider society. This can take a variety of forms. Laws which have developed out of and have meaning in one social and cultural context might very well have very little or no significance for those whose cultural, social, and religious background is very different and who have not internalized the norms the law is designed to protect. Again a society that places all the emphasis on the profit motive might well create value conflicts for those who believe that what counts above all else is the quality of the finished product, or a relaxed, tension-free atmosphere in which good human relations can thrive.

Then there is the possibility of finding that one has to live according to a set of norms and values which make very little sense or give very little meaning to one's life. This form of deprivation, labelled 'psychic', can give rise to the search for a new meaning system by means of which one can give coherence and order to one's life, explain and interpret it and in a sense control what happens. Finally, there is the possible disadvantage that can come from being ill or physically handicapped, amounting to what is termed organismic deprivation.[8]

To attempt to explain the rise of all the millenial movements of the kind we have been discussing purely in terms of one or other, or a combination, of the types of deprivation outlined above would be to oversimplify matters, and at the same time leave unanswered a number of important questions concerning the religious behaviour of both the privileged and the so-called deprived. Why, for example, do so many who appear to experience one or other, or a combination, of the above types of deprivation fail to resort to pre-millenialist forms of religion? Moreover, among those who feel deprived in one way or another some join highly pragmatic, this-worldly religious movements in the hope not of a profound, radical transformation of their present existence but more often in the hope of simply improving their present situation.

Paradoxically, it has sometimes been the case that when this improvement materializes radical, aggressive, protest movements, occasionally marked by millenial tendencies, emerge. One could cite as an example the Black Muslim movement, which became a nationally prominent sect in the United States in the late 1950s and appealed in the main to the relatively deprived — black migrants to the larger cities whose aspirations had been raised and sense of power enhanced. This movement developed a concept of salvation similar in many respects to the Rastafarian one. For the Black Muslim movement salvation rests upon a rediscovery of the traditions and a reconstruction of the history of the lost nation of Islam to which black people belong.[9] Like the Rastafarian movement, the Black Muslim movement is historically linked to Garveyism and the tradition of black protest in America already discussed. In this context it is worth mentioning that the father of one of its most important leaders, Malcolm X, was a Garveyite.

While deprivation cannot, therefore, provide us with a general explanation of millenial movements of the Rastafarian type it is not altogether irrelevant to an interpretation of the Rasta phenomenon. Rastafarians are not primarily seeking compensation for the relative economic and social deprivation they experience in Babylon, for they tend to shun the economic and social status concerns of white society; more fundamentally, it is a search for a relevant way of interpreting the past and present in the light of a future event. The movement, therefore, is very much concerned with developing a black understanding and interpretation of life and not simply with a search for techniques that will enable members to cope, or for recompense for the relative socio-economic deprivations which they experience in a society whose value system is predominantly European.

There is, however, a sense in which this movement is a religion of the deprived for it was in part born, as we have seen, out of a search for a lost cultural identity and awareness, a sense of dignity, self-respect and an appropriate and coherent system of values. And it is over against this background and the particular cultural and religious heritage of its members that the Rastafarian conception of sin and salvation needs to be examined and interpreted.

Rastafarian and African concepts of salvation. It seems appropriate here to compare, at the risk of over-generalization, the Rastafarian conception of salvation with that found in some new religions that began in Africa after the First World War and which are now to be found in many parts of Europe and North America.

But first a comment seems appropriate on the Rastafarian movement and what is usually referred to as African 'traditional' religion — by which is meant African belief systems as distinct from African Christianity and African Islam. There is, of course, no unified system of belief and practice that can be labelled 'African traditional religion' and applied to all the non-Christian, non-Muslim communities throughout Africa. Nevertheless, certain common characteristics can be identified, such as the widespread belief in a Supreme Being, the existence of lesser or subordinate gods, and in various kinds of sacrifice in the form of gift or thank offering, votive offering, propitiation and preventive sacrifice. Though not universal, the veneration of ancestors is also widespread, a practice which Rastafarians tend on the whole to repudiate.

The Rasfatarian notion of God (Jah) differs in certain respects from the idea of the High God as found in many African 'traditional' religions. Although regarded as the Creator, the King, omnipotent, immortal, the Judge, the Supreme Being in African traditional religious thought is sometimes seen as a withdrawn God who only intervenes in human affairs through his agents, the lesser gods. This is not the Rastafarian idea of God. Furthermore, although both the millenial theme and the notions of divine intervention to save mankind can both be found in African traditional religious thought, for example among the Lele of Zaire, [10] they do not usually occupy the same central position in the belief system as for Rastafarians. In most African traditional religions the emphasis is on the attainment of immediate goals both social and personal, such as a good harvest and protection from a certain disease or sickness. There is also the belief in an afterlife and in reincarnation, and while Rastafarians likewise believe in reincarnation they reject the notion of an afterlife. On the other hand, both the Rastafarian movement and African traditional religions are life-affirming and are not concerned in the traditional Christian or Muslim sense with salvation or immortality.

When we come to Africa's new religious movements, such as the Aladura (praying) churches which began to emerge in Nigeria in 1918 and which today have millions of adherents in West Africa and branches in all the main urban centres in Britain and many others in North America, we can detect here also a very pronounced life-affirming emphasis. Moreover, there is also a very deep concern with identity both at the personal and social levels, something already referred to in a previous chapter (see p. 55). Many of these African new religions, among them the Church of the Lord, the Cherubim and Seraphim Society, and the Brotherhood of the Cross and Star, all of Nigerian provenance, are concerned with the healing of sickness through prayer. They are in their central beliefs, orthodox Christian, believing in the power of Christ to conquer death, but often concentrate above all else on the healing power of his ministry. The stress on healing is but one indication that these new religions desire and work for the transformation of the world and not for escape from it. Another indication of this is their strong belief in a God who is closely involved in the world and in the affairs of men.

Furthermore, in some of these new movements, for instance in the Cherubim and Seraphim Society and the Church of the Lord, the emphasis as in the Rastafarian movement is on the God of the living and not of the dead, which is seen in, among other things, the exclusion of corpses from the church. [11] The theological reasons behind this repudiation of the dead, however, are not the same for the new African religions and the Rastafarians.

Again, in African new religions of the kind we have been discussing and in the Rastafarian movement there is a repudiation of a number of African rituals, including those associated with the veneration of ancestors, and an emphasis on food taboos. As with the Rastafarians, the Bible is given a central place in the life of these movements, informing and authenticating most of their beliefs and practices. But there also exists the belief that God has spoken anew to his African people in a 'new revelation' mediated through an African prophet.

This 'new revelation' does not make the Judaeo-Christian revelation obsolete but points rather to the fulfilment of that revelation for the people of Africa. As the Spirit of God was poured out on the Jewish people, and later on Christians at Pentecost, so it is now poured out again on the people of Africa through African prophets.

Sometimes, as in the case of Simon Kimbangu, prophet and founder of the Church of Jesus Christ on Earth, established in the former Belgian Congo (now Zaire) in 1921, the prophet comes to be closely identified with the Holy Spirit or Jesus Christ and is believed to dwell in the souls of the faithful, who believe that in every age God chooses someone from each race to enlighten and guide his people. Kimbangu is therefore the black Moses, the equivalent in the African context to Moses in relation to Israel, and a messianic figure of quasi-divine stature, not entirely unlike Haile Selassie as seen by the Rastafarians.

It is possible to find even in this very brief sketch of the perspectives and goals of African traditional religions and African new religious movements a number of similarities *and* differences, at the levels of belief and practice, between them and the Rastafarian movement, especially as far as the notions of sin and salvation are concerned. Despite the differences both in belief and practice, however, there is running through these African religious traditions and Rastafarians, a pronounced life-affirming, this-worldly orientation. Sin or evil is real and identifiable: salvation in practice consists for the most part in protecting members from this evil and in meeting their present needs, both spiritual and material, by recourse to supernatural agencies.

Other Rastafarian beliefs: Death.   The Rastafarian God (Jah), like the God of the new African religions, is a God of life, a living God who intends that man shall live forever. Death is possible, but only happens to those who shun righteousness. The righteous man, it is believed, cannot die and in a very 'unAfrican' way, excluding some of the African new religions discussed above, the Rastafarian purposely avoids any celebrations of death. In many African societies the death of a young person is marked by a display of deep sorrow and mourning; the death of a person of advanced age, however, is regarded differently: mourning is accompanied by great rejoicing to celebrate the fact that the person has lived out, so to speak, her/his natural span, triumphing over the hazards and dangers that lay in the way.

Rastafarians, on the other hand, do not usually attend other people's funerals, leaving the dead to bury the dead; nor, as we have seen, do they accept the Christian doctrine of death and afterlife, which they regard as a stratagem designed to create a sense of alienation and false consciousness by concentrating people's minds and attention on 'unreal' issues and problems. For them, the evil that causes death, and indeed all evil, can be expunged by 'knowing' righteousness and living naturally; that is, in accordance with the laws of nature.

One encounters a similar understanding of the cause of death and damnation in such movements as Rudolf Steiner's Anthroposophy and new religions of Indian provenance with a gnostic strain, which regard lack of 'knowledge', not sin in the Christian or Muslim understanding of the term, as the root of all evil. In these movements, as in the Rastafarian movement, the emphasis is on knowing, experiential knowledge, rather than on believing in divine truth.

Death, then, is unnatural and avoidable and, as far as the Rastas are concerned, it is an evil brought into their midst by foreign agents. The reflections, moreover, to which death gives rise are ones about immortality, 'natural' living, and punishment due to one who has failed to come to 'know' righteouness, bringing us to the Rastafarian notion of reincarnation.

Reincarnation. The belief in reincarnation is to be found in a number of African traditional religions, for example it is held by the Yoruba traditional religionists in south-western Nigeria and the Republic of Benin, as well as in Hinduism and Buddhism. It is a belief that is also taking hold in Christian and non-Christian circles in the West. [12] In the African setting, the newborn child is sometimes regarded as the reincarnation of an ancestor who desires to return to this life.

According to the Hindu doctrine of reincarnation the soul will return, in the perpetual round of *samsara* (rebirth), for a new life on earth; the nature and form this life takes will depend on one's past actions in a previous life. Thus one may 'return' by descending to animal life, or one may come back to another human life. Buddhist thought follows for the most part the Hindu concept of reincarnation.

The Rastafarians appear to have a more linear notion of rebirth. There is no question of going from one rebirth to another in a cycle. However, as in certain Hindu traditions, though not in Buddhism, the Rastafarians believe that from one rebirth to another the same person with the same identity, whatever the change in form, persists throughout. Thus all the 'black' prophets from Moses through Jesus to Haile Selassie are in this sense the same person.

This notion of reincarnation is central to the Rastafarian understanding of themselves as Africans and as the chosen people, the Israelites of the Old Testament. It is a belief, therefore, that points to the persistence of individual and racial identity despite the diaspora, enslavement and exile in Babylon.

A fragile belief system?   Much of what Rastafarians believe may strike some as pure myth or highly subjective nonsense which will be easily swept away when members emerge from the ghetto and confront the reality of everyday life. The whole thing is too fragile to be able to survive the buffeting it will inevitably be subjected to by everyday experience and rational explanation. The Rastafarians, it is suggested, will be shown to be mistaken about their own claims and beliefs as they confront the problem of protecting these in the light of the disconfirming evidence produced by historians and the harsh realities of everyday life, which is the lot of Ethiopians and many others in contemporary Africa. Rastafarian beliefs, indeed, could perhaps be regarded as even more fragile than most, since there is no institutional or organizational framework to foster these beliefs or protect them from external challenges.

To an extent Rastafarians have offset challenges to their beliefs and world-view by grounding them in their own interpretation of history, which is by no means as fragile as it might appear at first sight. It is an approach to history from an African perspective and though the intrepretation may not be shared by African historians, many would agree that the orientation is correct. Further it is a 'religious' view of history which many people, African or otherwise, would appreciate and even regard as more authentic and valid than 'secular' history.

Again, the Rastafarian approach to discerning truths, the intuitive, experiential path to understanding, supported by Scripture correctly understood, is in itself an approach that is far more widely accepted today than is often realized. In other words there is nothing terribly bizarre, unconventional, or 'misguided' about the foundation, sources, and method of validating Rastafarian belief. Rastas fully expect white society in particular to dismiss out of hand what they themselves 'know' to be the truth, which rather than disconfirming only serves to strengthen the conviction they have that they are right. As we shall see in the following chapter, Rastafarian beliefs are also protected by a specialized form of language, music, ritual and lifestyle, all of which serve to support the validity of the movement's claims.

One of the major strengths of the Rastafarian belief system may well lie in the fact that it lacks internal logical consistency and systematization. Today an increasing number of people appear to hold the view that in order to survive and appeal a church must offer an integrated, precise, consistent formulation of its teachings. There is great fear of the so-called liberal, middle-of-the-road, open-ended approach to belief and practice. Evangelicals and Fundamentalists share in common with converts to Churches of Satan the view that the symbolic approach to understanding truth is an abdication of authority on the part of Church leaders.

But there is no evidence to suggest that the highly systematic, logically consistent, literal presentation of doctrine is what a majority of people want or is any less fragile than a more imprecise, ambiguous, even inconsistent presentation. The fact that Rastafarian beliefs are not highly systematized or logically interconnected, and that they are capable of a number of possible interpretations, could well be a source of strength rather than an indication of their inherent fragility.

6

Rastafarian
Lifestyle and Rituals

Come, sit in the dust.
A Rasta invitation

The 'two great commandments' and the question of race. The Rastafarian movement is less about the acceptance of a set of doctrines and more about the way one lives; as one member expressed it, 'for the Rasta it is the way of life that is extremely important'.[1] But here again one should not search for complete uniformity, for a set pattern of behaviour and practice. There are, however, certain fundamental moral principles which most Rastas would strive to put into practice, beginning with the two 'great' commandments which enjoin love of God and love of neighbour. And these two commandments, along with the others, can be best kept in a 'natural' situation; that is, in a context in which living conforms to the laws of Nature. Before examining what is meant by 'living naturally', we can consider to what extent we can speak of love of God and love of neighbour as the twin pillars of Rastafarian morality, given its apparent emphasis on black superiority.

From Blyden onwards black spokesmen and leaders of the Back-to-Africa movements have sought to identify what is unique and distinctive about the African personality, and in some instances there is the suggestion that the black race is 'superior' in one respect or another to the white race and to people of mixed race such as mulattos, whom Blyden dismissed on one occasion as 'decadent'.[2]

Blyden strongly opposed any mixing of the races, and using the works of scientists, anthropologists, and even biblical texts, emphasized the fundamental importance and purpose of race preservation and development. God, he argued, created every race different and assigned each one a different task, creating the black race 'for the highest glory of all, which is the service of humanity'.[3] He made this appeal to all those who would seek to do away with the 'sentiment' of Race: 'honour your Race. Be yourselves, as God intended you to be or he would not have made you thus . . . if you are not yourself, if you surrender your personality, you have nothing left to give the world . . . '. And he added: 'Remember, then, that these racial peculiarities are God given . . . to neglect them, suppress them, or get rid of them is to get rid of the cord which binds us to the Creator.' [4]

For Blyden there was no incompatibility between his ideas on race preservation and the second of the two 'great commandments'. Indeed the development of the African personality, distinctive and unique in its own way, as other races were in theirs, was 'a way which fulfills the Second Commandment in the Law, which Christ says is like unto the first in importance. "Thou shall love thy neighbour as thyself" , ' [5]

While there are a number of what today would be termed racist comments in Blyden's writings, particularly as regards mulattos it is clear nonetheless that his determination to defend race integrity and race individuality was in no sense part of a philosophy of black, racial superiority developed with a view to legitimating black dominance over other races. Though he stressed that to abandon one's racial identity was 'the worst form of suicide', he also spoke of the need for co-operation between the different races and pointed out that no other race had anything to fear from the African engaged in fostering and developing his own personality and a sense of pride in his race. [6]

In essence Blyden's thesis was this: if the African were to allow himself to be influenced to such an extent by the West that he lost consciousness of his real identity and destiny as an African, then he would become simply an 'imitator' contributing nothing of his own or of value to human progress. For Blyden the highest peaks had been scaled by Europeans as far as scientific and technological development were concerned, but there was still much room for progress in the intellectual and spiritual spheres, and it was here that the African could make an important contribution, providing he refused to surrender his personality, for if he did so he would have nothing left to give the world. [7]

Without wishing to posit any direct link between Blyden's and Rastafarian thinking on race, they nevertheless have much in common. Some people, no doubt, will want to point to Rasta teaching about Babylon, discussed earlier (see Chapter 4), to Rasta songs, and practices which strike them as being racist in character and content. What, for example, is the observer to make of some of the 'protest and attack' songs and even of the so-called peace and love songs which certainly give the impression of excluding Europeans from among those who are to be counted as neighbours and loved. A line from one of the former type of songs reads: 'Wid a hammer and a rammer I will ram dem [Europeans] down', and in the words of one 'peace and love' song: 'Peace and love is based on love and justice. Europeans shall find no peace . . .'.

Moreover there are Rasta sects which exclude whites from membership on the grounds that the latter have no authentic African connection and cannot, therefore, participate fully in the movement. [8] Furthermore some Rastas themselves admit that the movement is not free of racism and that this is sometimes displayed against Europeans and Asians, and even against white Rastas. The more 'conscious' Rasta, however, sees it as a duty, a part of righteous living, to wrestle with racism and overcome it. [9]

Rastafarians also present themselves and, as Blyden did, the African race as a chosen race, along the same lines as the Jews; this, some may argue, is simply a sacralized form of racism. By way of contrast, the white man is depicted as wicked and evil and in many ways inferior to the black man. The latter was the first to be civilized, possesses greater and deeper knowledge than the white man, is and always has been closer to God, and one day in Ethiopia the blacks will be served by whites.

A form of inverted racism, perhaps, in response to history as briefly outlined in the earlier chapters of this book. This is part of the explanation, but once again it needs to be pointed out that there is no official or even uniform Rasta view on such matters as race or anything else. One can find as many, perhaps even more, 'positive' statements on race than 'negative' ones, such as the verse from one Rasta hymn which goes, 'Jah in the white, Jah in the black, Jah in the red. In any colour you want to name, Jah in him.' [10] For many Rastas, as for many Jewish people, the belief that they are a chosen race, a special people with a special mission who must not imitate the ways of other nations, has the connotation of special responsibility rather than favouritism. Like the Jews, Rastas see themselves as a 'covenant people', a people who have entered into an agreement with God which binds both parties. The agreement is conditional in that if one party is guilty of infidelity the other is released from its obligation. In fact the black race did from time to time, Rastas maintain, renege on its obligations, resulting in the disaster which overtook it in the form of the slave trade.

There is no doubt, however, that this concept of choice or election has caused problems and embarrassment, leading to charges of superiority, exclusivism, and racism. Whatever truth there may be in these allegations the reasons are more likely to be historical and sociological than doctrinal. A minority with a recent history so wretched as that of the Rastafarians is likely to react by demonstrating an attitude of exclusiveness and superiority, both of which are in some measure no more than defence mechanisms.

Colour in itself is not the main issue as far as many Rastafarians are concerned. As one Rasta expressed it, 'blackness is not about skin colour but about how one feels'.[11] And in the words of another, 'I and I [we] don't check for the skin anymore; we check for the spirit.'[12] If you experience 'black', approach life in the 'black' way, and are 'spiritually' African, then you are Rasta, and this is what 'serious' Rastas are concerned about. In the words of one white British Rasta: 'Some Rastas don't believe I can be a Rasta, but others say I have a black man's attitude to life, that I have learnt how to be spiritually one with them.'[13]

While they blame white society for most of the confusion, alienation, humiliation, and exploitation they and the black race have had to endure, Rastas are also highly critical of black people who have compromised themselves and become a party to exploitation and oppression. Among Rastafarians there is no straightforward, clear cut distinction between people based on colour, or a 'black is good', 'white is bad', mentality. Many affirm that all men, including the 'bald heads', those without locks, are children of God. Further, any Rastas seen abusing or attacking another person, in particular an old person, whether white or black, is liable to be taken away by a 'serious' Rasta and have his locks cut off for disgracing the movement.[14]

The Rastafarian movement is part of a long tradition of black protest that has offered a sharp challenge to white-dominated society, and it is this above all else that has served to create an image of it in the minds of some as a racist movement. There is in fact a resentment, even a hatred, of Babylon which has been raised to the level of a spiritual virtue in some Rastafarian quarters. Like the Black Muslim movement, the Rastafarians have divinized the black man, made him ruler of the universe, different only in degree from God himself.[15] But in practice the real concern of the 'serious' Rasta is not with revenge, destruction, or superiority, but with discovering the real self, and with constructing a more satisfying culture in which that self can be expressed.

Living 'naturally'.   Weary of living in exile in Babylon, Rastafarians long to return to Africa, their 'natural' abode, where they can live in full accordance with the laws of Nature. In Africa they can be close to their own people, their own culture and traditions. The fact that they are African means that they can only be fully themselves physically, emotionally, intellectually, and in every way in an African climate. In Africa, the Rasta believes, he will no longer be overshadowed by 'strangers' and prevented from realizing his true humanity, but being of the same race and mingling with the inhabitants of Africa will be strengthened and improved.

Living in accordance with Nature's laws, or living naturally, means, then, living in that climate and culture for which as an African, or a European, one is suited. For the Rasta it also means living in a society where Nature is respected, if not revered. Nature, or earth, is divine and obedience to its laws is the bedrock of morality and righteous living. An integral part of the Rasta quest consists of 'sitting in the dust', remaining close to the earth, the primary manifestation of Nature, in order to develop a deeper understanding of Nature's laws and be better equipped as a result to live in harmony with them.

In the West it is almost impossible now to 'sit in the dust', for there man confronts Nature, strives to manipulate and conquer it, disrespects its laws, is even prepared to manufacture weapons for the total destruction of this loving mother, earth. Africa, on the other hand, is held up as peace-loving, as a land without nuclear weapons, a place where Nature's laws are respected and obeyed. While he has reached unprecedented heights in science and technology, one consequence of which is the production of weapons of mass destruction, Western man is at the same time losing the ability 'to do for himself'. He has become almost totally dependent for his pleasure and comfort on 'artificial' techniques and gadgets which not only enslave him, both mentally and physically, but also cut him off from all real contact with nature. This, it is pointed out, was the downfall of the African who instead of 'doing for himself' once used slaves, as Western man now uses machines, to perform all his 'natural', normal, everyday tasks. This led to sloth, decadence, the inability to function naturally and normally, and so debilitated did the African become by cutting himself off from the earth that the European had no difficulty in enslaving him. [16]

In practice, living naturally means living on and off the land. It means producing one's own food 'naturally', eating only 'natural' (I-tal) food, and respecting the land's 'sacred' character by refusing to use it as a commercial commodity to be sold for profit. In all of this Rastas believe they are living both naturally and in the African way. As one observer comments: 'The Rastafarians acknowledge an urgent need to develop a culture which will restore to them the intimacy with nature which they knew in "ancient days".' [17]

Many Rastas feel that even if the climate were suitable they have no 'space' to live 'naturally' in the West, where consumerism dominates everything. Without land, they are forced to buy and sell Nature's products. And then the consumption of 'I-tal' or natural, organic food, poses a problem in hospitals, institutions of education,

Rastafarian couple, south-east London (*J. Allan Cash Photolibrary*)

prisons and elsewhere, and is compounded by the fact that people are often unaware of Rastafarian custom and practice, or are reluctant to take them seriously on matters of diet, even though it is clear from research that some Rastas hold strictly to the movement's dietary rules. These consist basically of avoiding swine's flesh, alcohol, and all food prepared by non-members and from unknown sources. Rastas are to all intents and purposes vegetarians.

While the Rasta style of life and moral code are said to give 'inner strength and security' and are the 'nearest thing to enabling a person to be content with himself', it can be a difficult life, especially in Britain. It involves confrontation with others in that the Rasta has to decide to wear locks, to dress and live the way he does, while knowing that others, both black and white, do not accept him. Moreover 'serious' Rastas are aware that things are made even more difficult by the fact that others dress in Rasta style, and behave in a non-Rasta fashion while claiming, in the hope of being shielded by the 'religion', to be Rastas.

Despite the difficulties a number of Rastas have committed themselves to the task of creating 'space' for themselves in Babylon. They seek to transform white society so that they will be free to live 'naturally' in that society and are convinced this is possible. In the words of one Rasta who supports this approach: 'If I and I [we] believe very strongly, we can live here how I and I [we] wish.'[18] If this approach were to become dominant, then any emphasis on exclusiveness and hostility to whites would inevitably be modified since it would constitute an argument not for separation but for pluralism, which in turn would require mutual respect and interaction. This may explain, further, the frequent references made in more recent times in certain Rasta quarters to Haile Selassie's condemnation of the idea of racial segregation.

The role of the 'queens'. In the opinion of some observers women are treated very much as an inferior species in the Rastafarian movement. According to one researcher who focused on the situation in Jamaica, 'The problematic of female-male dynamics in Rastafarian culture are evident in all societies. In Rasta, however, we find a highly polarized version of them. While many liberation movements have an ideology of egalitarianism but in fact practise sexual hierarchy, the Rastafarian movement, in addition to the espousal of universal human values actually has developed an explicit ideology about the subordination of women.'[19]

One can point to a number of movements, including the American Left movement in 1960s and 1970s, American black movements, and the Algerian Liberation Movement, in which women were allegedly

Rasta father with child, Brixton, London (*J. Allan Cash Photolibrary*)

subordinated to men. In the Rastafarian movement, it has been suggested, 'women are not able to share equally in defining' the developments which the movement seeks to bring about.[20] While the movement, operating according to patriarchal principles and a 'clearly defined sexual division of labour', offers women a degree of security and stability in a chaotic, sometimes anomic situation and therefore might appeal to them for these reasons, women play little part in reasoning sessions and are 'tolerated if they accepted the male definition of the situation'.[21]

Rastafarian attitudes towards women differ little, if at all, from those found generally in Jamaican society and 'mirror the culture of the European colonizers to whom they are ideologically opposed'.[22] At the same time, women 'are eulogized as symbolically equivalent to Mother Africa', and there exists in Rastafarian ideology 'a Utopian conception of the ideal woman'.[23] While Rasta men present a dignified image of women, they also hold to the view that the woman's way to 'salvation' is through man. A fallen creature, the woman — referred to as sister, daughter, or queen — needs to be guided and controlled by the man, the king.

Other writers say relatively little about the role of women in the movement and tend to suggest that, while it is a subordinate one, women accept this with conviction, supporting their rejection of feminism and women's liberation with quotations from the Bible. Did not God create man in his own image and woman to be his companion?[24]

In much of the literature on the Rastafarian movement, with one or two notable exceptions, the idealized, utopian model of woman is the one presented, and it is the one which both male and female members in Britain accept and regard as authentic. Rasta women interviewed, among them a former university student, did not feel in any way aggrieved or dissatisfied with their situation. Extremely articulate and open to discussion on a person to person basis, women interviewed in the company of men usually sat in the background and said little or nothing about themselves or about the movement. However, one occasionally encounters women who, even in the presence of their male partners, take a strong feminist line and challenge anything which smacks of sexism. There are also those who argue that, even if it could be proved that Rasta men are sexist, the struggle against racism must take priority over all else.

Rasta men interviewed point to the fact that they refer to their women partners as queens, and that this is not only an accolade but illustrates that a Rasta man does not seek to own or possess his partner. Rasta men, further, attach great importance to sharing their life with their children, to staying at home with them, to being with them. Family life, furthermore, and the extended family system in particular, is highly regarded, though marriage is not usually formalized and solemnized in the Western, Christian way. Abortion and contraception are rejected, some going so far as to maintain that these are two of the means devised by white society for the purpose of eliminating the black race.

From an outsider's perspective it would seem that Rasta men, however noble an image they might have of their 'queens', exclude them from decision-making and value them above all else as followers and mothers. Women, however, are not in practice confined to the home and often taken on the role of breadwinner, going out to work while the man stays at home to look after the children. When outside the home women cover their heads and dress modestly; as one explained, 'we dress like Muslim women'.

The Rastafarian way of life, then, is in principle about living naturally, about 'sitting in the dust' and spreading love and peace to all. It is opposed to physical violence, whether for purposes of destroying Babylon or teaching children to live righteously. The aim of this way of life is spiritual revolution, which involves an entire reconstruction of the way one thinks about and understands the meaning and purpose of life, a revolution already begun by those who pray, meditate, 'reason' and cultivate locks.

Reasoning sessions. The main Rastafarian rituals consist of daily prayers, meditation, and meetings or reasoning sessions. While there is no obligation to pray daily, many Rastas petition Haile Selassie in the following or a similar way each day: 'So we hail our God, Selassie-I, Eternal God, Ras Tafari, hear us and help us and cause Thy face to shine upon us, Thy children.' Some not only pray daily but also meditate or 'head rest with Jah', desirous to know the inner self, to understand 'the book within', which contains divine revelation.

At meetings or reasoning sessions, also known as groundings, which Rastas prepare for by strict adherence to moral and dietary rules, brethren tell one another of the revelations they have received during meditation or in dreams. It is at these sessions that brethren ritually smoke the 'sacred chalice' or 'holy herb' ganja (marijuana). The sessions take place whenever the brethren feel they should, are held in a commune or yard and are presided over by an elder. Numbers can vary from no more than a handful to several hundred depending on the occasion. Drum playing, ritual chanting, hymns, lyrics, and poetry create the 'religious' atmosphere in which the 'chalice' is taken and the 'reasoning' carried on.

Ganja smoking. While there is no obligation to participate in the smoking of ganja most of the brethren do take the 'chalice', that is the cow-horn pipe in which it is passed around from member to member and offered to all, including children. It is also smoked in other ways; for example, in the form of a rather large, rolled cigarette. The remains of what is left of the substance is sometimes used to make tea, or simply rubbed into the skin for purposes of healing.

Ganja in fact is regarded as a source of revelation, inspiration, nutrition, relaxation, entertainment, and healing. Many illnesses are treated by recourse to the 'herb' or 'weed', two more of ganja's many names, and support for its use is to be found, Rastas claim, in the Bible, in particular in Genesis 1: 29, Psalm 18: 18, and Revelation 22: 2. Before the cup is taken silence reigns, brethren take off their hats, and pray to the 'God within' whom they are about to worship and praise. It is further believed that this is the most natural way to worship God since it involves the use of natural products of which ganja is one of the most widespread in Jamaica.

Ganja is also smoked at other times, and almost always for a combination of different reasons. One Rasta smokes it becasue 'I enjoy it, and for meditation and social reasons'. Some smoke it almost all the time, maintaining that by so doing they remain constantly aware of who they are and where they are going.

There are those, however, who object to ganja being used in this way, arguing that if used constantly and uninterruptedly it is likely to become an end in itself rather than a means of opening up the self to discover one's true, inner nature. In the words of one Rasta, 'Ganja is correctly used when Rastas wish to become more aware, more receptive, when one wants to assimilate something one has just heard or read or seen, and this is best done in groups, at reasoning sessions.' It is pointed out that ganja smoking can be dangerous, and that the 'weed' should only be taken by a person who is 'at one with himself otherwise he will be unable to cope with the feelings produced, and unable to channel them positively'. [25]

Cultivating locks. Like the use of ganja the cultivation or growing of locks, known as dreadlocks, is seen as biblically inspired and also in accordance with the laws of nature. Referring to the Book of Numbers, Rastas quote the verses which read, 'As long as he is bound by his vow, no razor shall touch his head; until the time of his consecration to Yahweh is completed, he remains under vow and shall let his hair grow free' (6: 5-6). Here we have a Rasta image of themselves as consecrated people who have entered into a covenant with God, one of the signs of which is the cultivation of dreadlocks.

Locks also symbolize strength, and in this respect are a reminder of the power of Samson's hair which enabled him to destroy the Philistines. By the cultivation of locks Rastafarians identify not only with Old Testament warriors such as Samson, but also with African peoples, among them the Galla and Masai people of Eastern Africa, though it is worth pointing out here that in some parts of Africa long hair that gives the appearance of being unkempt is traditionally regarded as a sign of mental disorder.[26] Dreadlocks, however, are often shaped and styled, the shapes and models being inspired by the head and mane of the lion — the Lion of Judah being one of Haile Selassie's titles. To Rastafarians the lion symbolizes strength and vigour, so that it can be said of themselves and their leader: 'Lo, the people riseth up as a lioness and as a lion doth he range through the land.' On the Apocalyptic model, Haile Selassie as Lion of Judah has the special power to overcome and to make obscure matters plain by opening the sealed book containing the secrets of life. A roaring lion, who controls the animal and human world, he rouses the African from a deep sleep and is the sign of a new, vigorous life, of a resurrection of the African race.

The Rastafarian not only cultivates dreadlocks to resemble thereby the head and mane of the lion, the royal symbol of the vigour and enterprise of the black race, but also imitates this animal's regal, dignified walk, manifesting to others that despite enslavement and oppression he belongs to a princely race with a glorious past. Dreadlocks then are a device for stimulating a greater self-awareness, a deeper consciousness of the Rasta's origins, and also of his present condition. Tired with attempting to conform to the lifestyle, standards and norms of white society, a conformism which, it was judged, only served to weaken their sense of identity without guaranteeing respect and acceptance, Rastas have decided to explain to the wider society who and what they are by a form of symbolic confrontation.

By cultivating dreadlocks Rastas distance themselves from the wider society, at the same time signalling that they have no wish to be accepted or respected if this means conforming to the latter's criteria. The message is that they are either appreciated for what they are — that is, as Africans with a long history and civilization of which they have been and continue to be deprived — or not at all. In this way Rastas not only decide the criteria by which they should be judged by others, but also increase their marginality. This, however, is not incompatible with either their belief in the imminent collapse of Babylon or their hope of repatriation. Rastas have situated themselves in the 'wilderness': given their beliefs, way of life, and interpretation of history, this is an appropriate place to be. The cultivation of

Dreadlocks (*J. Allan Cash Photolibrary*)

dreadlocks is intended to symbolize this historical stage of wandering through the wilderness towards the promised land.

The vow not to allow a razor to touch the head and to let the hair grow free is also a response to slavery and oppression in that it manifests a total rejection of the notion of the black person as simply an economic commodity, a mere unit of labour, who can be bought and sold, and whipped and flogged at the whim of a master bent on profiting from slave labour. Rasta songs tell of the physical violence inflicted on black people during the era of slavery, in particular of the desecration by whips and sharp instruments of their bodies, to say nothing of mental enslavement; it is against this background that the Rasta decision to let their hair and beard grow free and, in the words of Leviticus, to 'avoid making any cuttings in the flesh' (21: 5) should be understood.

Thus in the cultivation of dreadlocks and the growth of long beards — some can be several feet long — there is an effort to create a set of positive, African values with which black people can identify. But while the intention and aim might find acceptance among some black people, the cultivation of locks and Rastafarian symbols and rituals are not only ambiguous but also in flat contradiction to other black people's experience and knowledge of African customs, traditions and values, unless the Rastas are seen by them as prophetic figures.

Language.   Rasta language or patois is no less important in fostering an awareness of individual and group identity and in creating a set of positive values than the cultivation of locks. The most obvious indication of this from the language point of view is the wide use made of the personal pronoun 'I'. This forms either the prefix or suffix to a whole range of words which in the words of one observer, 'continually recall to the Rasta the importance of his own personhood and that of Jah'. [27]

Treated as less than human, as mere units of labour, the black person must constantly remind himself, the Rasta believes, that he is a human being, a person of value and worth and not a mere 'slave by nature'. This accounts for the frequent use of the pronoun 'I'. Very often a Rasta will substitute '*I-n-I*' for we, and '*I*' for me, and words such as receive will be altered to *I-ceive,* desire to *I-sire,* create to *I-rate*, Amen to *I-men*. There are many more of these 'I-words', including personal names, and almost always the 'I' is placed after the name of the messiah, which then reads *Haile-Selassie-I.*

While in large measure Jamaican from the point of view of syntax and grammar, Rastafarian speech has developed this distinctive characteristic for the purpose of protecting self-identity and avoiding language that might contribute to further servility, self-degradation, or objectification of the person. Rasta language also sustains Rastafarian reality, affirming and reinforcing what the 'members' stand for and the social identity and order they seek to create. It is, moreover, a force for greater cohesion and solidarity, while at the same time it defines the boundary between Rastas and non-Rastas.

Language, or more precisely words, are also a source of great power, opening up pathways to the inner self, to ultimate reality. One finds the same belief in the power of words in many African religious traditions, and indeed in virtually all religious traditions. Among the Rastafarians language, and also music, not only act to generate and sustain belief and respect, allowing them to be themselves, but also possess a power greater than that of death: simply calling on or chanting the name of Haile Selassie the Rasta resurrects him.

Rasta music's religious ('churchical') character. This music was first recorded in 1960 by the Rastafarian drummer Count Ossie, and in turn influenced the Ska musicians or Skatalities, Ska having evolved out of the impact of American rhythm and blues on mento, a Jamaican equivalent of the rumba and calypso. Ska was superseded by the slower blue beat or rock-steady music, which combined mento and soul music; reggae developed in a big way in the late 1960s through bands like the Upsetters and Toots, the Maytals, Jimmy Cliff, and the Wailers. Bob Nesta Marley (See chapter 4, pp. 52-3) was signed up by the Wailers in 1973, and in 1974 *Catch a Fire* was released; from then until his death from cancer in 1981 Marley's stature grew enormously in Jamaica and around the world. [28]

Identified by its popular rhythms (ridims) and three Rasta drums, the bass, fundeh and repeater, all painted in the red, green, gold and black colours of the movements, Rasta music was influenced in its early stages in the 1940s by Pukkumina, Kumina, and revivalist groups (see Chapter 1, pp. 25-6), all operating the same social context in West Kingston, Jamaica. The Rastas, while appreciating the links between these groups and Africa, rejected their use of music and dance to evoke spirit possession and found that they had more in common with the Burru people, who strongly believed in maintaining their African roots, particularly in the field of music.

These influences apart, Rasta music was developed at 'reasoning sessions', at which, in the words of its pioneer Count Ossie, brethren discussed 'Garveyism, Rastafarianism and the whole question of Black awareness'. [20] At these sessions Count Ossie expressed the view that the black race should develop its own music, as other races had done. African music, of course, has a much longer history than this. However, in Jamaica Burru drumming was one of the most 'authentic' forms of African music still in existence in the 1940s, and was adopted, developed, and used at reasoning sessions.

The music had then, and still has, a religious ('churchical') purpose, enabling brethren to 'reason' more clearly and in greater depth, and in this way to discover the answers to the many questions that they posed concerning their own identity and purpose as black people. Religious significance, moreover, is attached to the drums, something one finds among, for example, the Yoruba people of south-western Nigeria and Benin (Dahomey). The drums and the rhythms (ridims) create in the Rastafarian a sense of his African identity, reinforce their moral, ethical, doctrinal, and social values and protect them from alienation and false consciousness. The music also helps in the struggle against 'downpression', depression, which comes from living in Babylon, and acts generally as a vehicle for the release of inner tension.

Rasta music, it is believed, has the power to heal not only mentally but also physically, driving away colds, fevers and headaches. It is also performed for pleasure, or as it is sometimes put, for 'eartical' and 'heartical' reasons. But music is always intended to serve a religious purpose, to generate 'religious' feeling and upliftment in individuals, to foster a spiritual bond among the brethren, to facilitate by 'natural ridim' natural living, to praise and worship Jah, to commune with Him, and to spread His word.

Rasta songs and hymns also express sentiments of love, hope and confidence, revenge, hostility, and protest. However, not all the lyrics and melodies used by Rastas are their own. Some of the songs are sung to the tune of 'western', Christian hymns like 'The Church is One Foundation'. Others like 'Holy Mount Zion', are Rasta creations and express the desire for repatriation, understood in a variety of different senses by members:

> I want to go to Mount Zion
> I want to go to Mount Zion, I
> Singing, Holy, holy, holy,
> Holy, holy, holy,
> Holy, Mount Zion.

Within hymn and song Rastas re-live the 'call' to return to their African heritage and way of natural living, and reaffirm their rejection of Babylon.

7

From Self-awareness to the Brotherhood of Man

They know who they are.
A non-Rasta Ethiopian

Rastafarians have never sought to be accepted by the wider society where acceptance has meant conformity. That would be to undermine the whole purpose of being a Rasta, which is to 'live naturally' in the African way, and to make Ethiopia, symbolic of Africa and all things African, the centre of their universe. This is seen as an essential prerequisite of self-realization; to seek acceptance by conforming to the standards and norms of Babylon is simply to perpetuate a process begun with slavery and continued during the era of colonialism and neo-colonialism, which if not reversed will result in total 'loss of memory' and therefore of that which makes an individual and a people what they are.

The cultivation of locks, as we have seen, is regarded as biblically inspired and in accordance with the laws of nature; but also, like the Rasta dress and lifestyle generally, it is meant to shock the wider society into recognizing and eventually accepting that Rastas are different and more precisely that they are a people, a race, with their own customs, history, culture and world view which ought to be taken seriously and never allowed to perish. As one Rasta expressed it: 'I and I [we] know that in dressing like this I and I will be regarded as mad, dangerous and all that . . . but I and I don't care for I and I want freedom for all people to be themselves.' [1]

Rastas, and they are by no means alone in this, pose a fundamental question: what sort of life, what sort of a world, and above all what sort of self can survive and be sustained that has no memory of its own past and of its moorings in time? As Buñuel puts it, 'You have to begin to lose your memory if only in bits and pieces, to realize that memory is what makes our lives. Life without memory is no life at all . . . Without it we are nothing.' [2]

This is an essential part of the Rasta message. Belief in the divinity of Haile Selassie is undoubtedly very important for many Rastas, but what is even more important is to avoid becoming a people without a past of their own, stuck in a constantly changing, meaningless moment. This explains the Rasta preoccupation with the royal lineage of Haile Selassie, traced back as far as Solomon and beyond, and with Old Testament history in general. Herein, it is believed, lie the foundations of black history, the history of a chosen race which, being divinely inspired, is beyond all dispute. Convinced that the 'true' African past has been completely distorted for the purpose of justifying slavery and colonialism, and that in the process Africans have been 'de-souled' and the memory of themselves as a sophisticated, civilized, and cultured people destroyed, Rastas seek continuity and reality with their African past in their lifestyle, music, art, rituals, and beliefs. There they rediscover their soul and their memory, in a similar way to those Africans, enslaved in the Caribbean and the Americas, who through African traditional religious beliefs and rituals kept alive the memory of their homeland. [3]

Certainly, whatever else they may think of Rastafarian ideas and practices, many of the black youth in Britain, France, the United States and elsewhere, find Rastas more aware, more confident and sure of themselves than many Africans. Informants from among the non-Rasta black community in Britain speak of them as being 'generally quietly confident, relaxed, sure of their identity'. [4] In the words of one Ethiopian, not himself a Rasta but who knows many of the brethren, 'The Rastas know who they are'. [5]

The Rastas, however, have many critics and generally the response from all sections of British society has been unsympathetic. To repeat Lord Scarman's point: 'The Rastafarians, their faith and their aspirations, deserve more understanding and more sympathy than they get from the British people.' [6] In Britain, and elsewhere, Rastas are understandably seen as a threat to established norms and values, since all societies find it difficult and unnerving to have to cope with ideas and ways of behaving that refuse to fit in with their experiences and long established pattern of assumptions. Other issues, such as racism and the very fact that the Rastas themselves do not look for or encourage a sympathetic response, also determine the reaction of the wider society. None of this, however, can be made an excuse for the indiscriminate stopping and questioning of Rastas in the streets. As Lord Scarman made clear 'The true Rastafarian accepts the law of the land'. [7] Unfortunately others not themselves Rastas dress as such simply to be fashionable, and when challenged by the police for drug peddling, for example, explain that they are Rastas and are only following their religion. In Britain, in fact, it is now no longer possible to tell Rastas simply by their appearance.

The Rastafarian movement has changed over time moving from an exclusivist, introversionist position with regard to white society to one which increasingly emphasizes 'the brotherhood of man under the fatherhood of God', [8] a shift in perspective and attitude expressed more pointedly and graphically by the Rasta who, in explaining that Haile Selassie opposed the idea of racial segregation, commented: 'I and I [we] don't check for the skin anymore; I and I check for the spirit.' [9]

This desire to transcend the divisions of race by encouraging and fostering belief in a universal spirit does not preclude in the Rasta view the development and heightening of race consciousness and awareness among Africans and people of African descent, nor the quest for African unity. Like Blyden, Garvey, and others before them, it would seem that many Rastas today in cultivating the sense and experience of being African are striving not only to eradicate all feeling of inferiority among Africans and to protect their African identity but also to find a solution to the complex problems which have arisen as a result of the contact between western and African cultures. In relatively recent times, in other contexts and from a somewhat different starting point, a great deal of African literature has addressed itself to this very problem, one of the best known works on this subject being Chinua Achebe's novel *Things Fall Apart.*

In this literature, as in the writings of Blyden when taken as a whole, the central point is not the avoidance of contact between the black and white races but rather the contribution each race can make in its own way to the peace and progress of human civilization. As we have seen, Blyden's aim in developing a philosophy of 'African-ness', in attempting to re-establish the psychic and emotional security of Africans undermined by slavery and colonization, and in developing to the full a distinctive African personality, was, as much as anything else, an attempt to dispel false notions and myths in wide circulation about Africa as the 'dark', 'benighted' continent. This view of Africa still exists today, even among people of African descent. When asked about their views on the Rastafarian movement a number of West Indians in London began by saying that 'they [the Rastas] are the people who want to return to the 'dark' continent'. [10]

Rastas today, it would seem, are involved in much the same enterprise as Blyden, though it would be misleading to suggest that they are unique in this. There have been a number of successful attempts to encourage Africans and others to look at the world from an African perspective, and perhaps none more so than the distinguished university of Ibadan (Nigeria) school of history. What the Rastas have done, and continue to do, in ways by no means acceptable to all Africans, is to take this message to the inner cities of the western world. In London, Paris, Bordeaux, and other European cities with a large black population, Rastas are encouraging other Africans to express openly and unreservedly their 'African-ness'.

Rastas are also being influenced and are learning a great deal from other Africans whom they encounter in these cities. In Paris and Bordeaux, for example, they have come to learn from the Senegalese there about Ahmadu Bamba, founder of the Mouride brotherhood [11] and regarded today by many in Senegal and other former West African states as a hero and freedom fighter who, although he never took up arms to defend his country, nevertheless in other ways strongly resisted the French penetration and colonization of Senegal. In France Rastas now chant not only 'Jah, Jah, Jah', but also 'Bamba, Bamba, Bamba' as part of their consciousness-raising strategy. [12]

While the Rastafarian movement is not the first black movement of its kind it is creating something new, especially for those young black people in, for example, London who feel neither British nor West Indian. To these people in particular the movement gives strength and a sense of identity. In ancient Ethiopia, symbol of a free and independent Africa, they find pride and achievement for, as Rastas say, 'It relates to I and I'.

To some outside observers the movement may well appear to be nothing more than an irrational, whimsical outbreak of millenial rhetoric and fantasizing, and to others an obstacle to the development of a multi-racial, multi-cultural society. The movement appears to represent at one level a total rejection of white society and its definition of reality and a determined effort to generate in the minds of black people a hatred of Babylon matched only by a love and adulation for all things African. Instead of seeking an objective, critical understanding of their African past, Rastas seem to prefer to ground themselves in a mythical interpretation of that past, which they not only hold to with utter certainty but also sanctify and legitimate by their own peculiar approach to Scripture, leaving no room for open discussion and debate with others who do not share their views of life.

If this was the true picture there would be little prospect of co-operation in the interests of a multi-cultural, multi-racial society; but despite the fact that some of the brethren place great emphasis on physical repatriation to Africa and shun all contact with Babylon, the Rastafarian movement as a whole could be, paradoxically, a con-structive, innovative force as far as social integration is concerned. The restoration and revitalization of the African past, the 'natural living', the belief in Haile Selassie as the messiah, and the enthusiasm for Africana in general, all help to provide those who feel rejected by white society and who have no experience of Africa, with a memory of who they are and where they belong, and with the basis both of an identity and an image of themselves which they themselves have created: both are necessary preconditions for their participation in a multi-cultural society.

Perhaps the paradox is resolved by noting that an increasing number of Rastafarians have shifted away from the goal of total separation and physical repatriation, from hostility to white society, to an emphasis on pluralism which is not in fact separatism but a form of integration requiring mutual respect and involving considerable interaction. At least some of the developments mentioned in this book point in that direction. Increasingly Rastas are more concerned with creating their own identity than with separation and see their efforts in this direction as pro-black rather than anti-white.

Similar developments have taken place within the Black Muslim movement in the United States; like the latter, the Rastafarian movement represents an attempt to 'heal the wound of dual membership' in white dominated society. [13] Within the context of the movement self-pride and shaken confidence have been restored, a fact attested to by both members and observers alike.

This, however, is not to suggest that the Rastafarian way is the only way, or even the most appropriate and effective way, of meeting the existential needs of those who take it up. Who can say whether Rastas might not be more successful in achieving their goals were they to follow another path? 'Success' and 'failure' in these matters, however, are hardly appropriate concepts for the social historian. All we can say is that many of those who have observed Rastas and know them well are impressed by their calm, self-confidence derived from their unshakeable certainty that 'Jah live'.

This certainty persists, despite such catastrophies as the recent famine in Ethiopia which some Rastas claim to have predicted and which others explain away as simply another example of Babylonian exploitation designed to secure an even tighter grip on Africa. For some, however, the famine has made it abundantly clear that 'physical' repatriation to Ethiopia cannot be the ultimate aim of their quest.

While Ethiopia, the only African country never to be formally colonized, remains for all Rastafarians the 'oldest spiritual home of God on earth', and stands for 'all of Africa when free', it has increasingly come to symbolize any situation or place in which the constraints imposed by Babylon have been removed, thereby allowing Rastas the freedom to live naturally in the African way. It would seem to follow that for the many Rastas who hold this view 'Ethiopia' can be created in any society and that repatriation is less about the actual, physical return of Rastas to Africa and more about the restoration of shattered pride and self-confidence.

Notes

INTRODUCTION

1 K. Knott, *My Sweet Lord: The Hare Krishna Movement* (Wellingborough: The Aquarian Press, 1986).

2 P. B. Clarke, 'New Paths to Salvation', *Religion Today,* Vol. 1, No. 1 (May 1984), 2.

3 R. Littlewood and M. Lipsedge, *Aliens and Alienists. Ethnic Minorities and Psychiatry*, (Harmondsworth, Middlesex: Penguin Books, 1982).

4 Hans Mol, *Identity and the Sacred* (Oxford: Basil Blackwell, 1976).

5 E. U. Essien-Udom, *Black Nationalism: A Search for Identity in America* (Chicago: University of Chicago Press, 1962); G. E. Simpson, *Black Religions in the New World* (New York: Columbia University Press, 1978).

6 M. Calley, *God's people. West Indian Pentecostal Sects in England* (Oxford: Oxford University Press, 1965); C. Hill, *Black Churches. West Indian and African Sects in Britain* (British Council of Churches, 1971).

7 There is some speculation about the existence of a Black Pentecostalist church in London from around 1908, but to my knowledge, no hard evidence has so far been found to support this claim. This, however, is not to suggest that either the evidence has not been found or does not already exist.

8 R. Gerloff in 'The Development of Black Churches in Britain since 1952', paper presented to the conference on 'The Development and Impact of New Religious Movements' at King's College, London, 18-19 April 1983, estimated that there were 185 of these churches.

9 T. Booth, *We True Christians,* Ph.D, Thesis, University of Birmingham, 1984. This is an anthropological account of the Church of the Cherubim and Seraphim begun in Birmingham in 1969 by a Nigerian student, and which subsequently attracted a large following from among the West Indian as well as the Nigerian population of that city.

10 F. M. Mbon, 'A New Typology for Africa's New Religious Movements', in *Update*, Vol. 8, Nos. 3-4 (September/December 1984), 35-43.

11 B. R. Wilson, *Religious Sects* (London: Weidenfeld, 1970).

12 J. Owens, *Dread. The Rastafarians of Jamaica* [with an introduction by Rex Nettleford] (London: Heinemann Education Books 1979), p. 71 and *passim*.
13 L. Barrett, *The Rastafarians. The Dreadlocks of Jamaica* (London: Heinemann 1977), p. 2.
14 Lynch, op. cit., p. 65.
15 Quotation from R. W. July, *The Origins of Modern African Thought* (New York: Praeger, 1967), p. 233.
16 G. Shepperson, 'Notes on Negro American Influences On The Emergence of African Nationalism', *Journal of African History*, 1, 2 (1960), 301.
17 Lynch, op. cit., p. 67.
18 B. Sundkler, *Bantu Prophets in South Africa* [2nd edition] (London: Oxford University Press for the International African Institute, 1961), pp. 39-40.
19 E. A. Ayandele, *The Missionary Impact on Modern Nigeria 1842-1914* (London: Longman, 1966), p. 177.
20 A. Raboteau, *Slave Religion,* op. cit. p. 312.

CHAPTER 1

1 Britain has the largest number of Rastafarians outside Jamaica.
2 R. N. Bellah in *Religion and Progress in Modern Asia* (New York: Free Press, 1965), p. 23.
3 J. E. Inikori, Introduction to *Forced Migration. The Impact of the Export Slave Trade on African Societies* (London: Hutchinson University Library, 1981).
4 P. D. Curtin, *The Atlantic Slave Trade: A Census* (Madison: University of Wisconsin Press, 1969), p. 91.
5 W. L. Williams, *Black Africans and the Evangelization of Africa, 1877-1900* (Madison: University of Wisconsin Press, 1982), pp. 6 ff.
6 Ibid.
7 R. Littlewood and M. Lipsedge, *Aliens and Alienists. Ethnic Minorities and Psychiatry* op. cit., p. 45.
8 Aristotle, *The Politics,*. T. A. Sinclair (Harmondsworth Middlesex: Penguin Books), 1962, pp. 30 ff.
9 G. E. Simpson, *Black Religions in the New World* New York: Columbia University Press, 1978), pp. 26 ff.
10 Ibid., p. 29.
11 A. J. Raboteau, *Slave Religion. The 'Invisible Institution' in the Antebellum South* (Oxford: Oxford University Press, 1980), p. 144.
12 Ibid., p. 147.
13 C. K. G. Gwassa, 'Kinjikitile and the Ideology of Maji-Maji', in T. O. Ranger and I. Kimambo (eds.), *A Historical Study of African Religion* (London: Heinemann, 1972), pp. 202-19.
14 L. E. Barrett, *The Rastafarians. The Dreadlocks of Jamaica* (Kingston: Sangster's Book Stores Ltd. in Association with Heinemann, 1977), p. 40.

15 Ibid., p. 50.
16 Ibid., pp. 24-5.

CHAPTER 2

1. P. B. Clarke, *West Africa and Christianity* (London: Edward Arnold, 1985), chap. 2; C. Fyfe, *A History of Sierra Leone* (London: Oxford University Press, 1962); J. Peterson, *Province of Freedom* (Evanston, Ill: Northwestern University Press, 1969); L. Sanneh, *West African Christianity* (London: C. Hurst, 1983).
2 T. W. Schick, *Behold The Promised Land* (Baltimore and London: Johns Hopkins University Press, 1977).
3 H. R. Lynch, *Edward Wilmot Blyden. Pan-Negro Patriot 1832-1912* (London: Oxford University Press, 1967).
4 Ibid., p. 10.
5 R. W. July, *The Origins of Modern African Thought. Its Development in West Africa During the Nineteenth and Twentieth Centuries* (New York: Praeger, 1967).
6 Ibid.
7 Lynch, op. cit., p. 55.
8 E. W. Blyden, *Christianity, Islam and the Negro Race* (Edinburgh: Edinburgh University Press, 1967).
9 Lynch, op. cit., p. 55.
10 Ibid., p. 57.
11 Ibid., p. 55.
12 Ibid., p. 60.
13 E. W. Blyden, 'Africa for the Africans', *African Repository* XLVIII, in H. R. Lynch (ed.) *Blyden, Black Spokesman. Selected Published Writings* (London: Cass, 1971).

CHAPTER 3

1 Lynch, *Edward Wilmot Blyden*, op. cit., p. 121.
2 Shepperson, *Notes on Negro American Influences*, op. cit., p. 300.
3 Ibid.
4 *Autobiography of Kwame Nkrumah* (Edinburgh: T. Nelson and Sons Ltd., 1957), p. 45.
5 Ibid., p. 184.
6 Gunnar Myrdal, *An American Dilemma* (New York: Harper, 1944), p. 749.
7 Williams, *Black Americans and the Evangelization of Africa*, op. cit., p. 50.
8 Ibid.
9 Ibid., p. 52.
10 Ibid., p. 100.
11 Ibid.
12 Shepperson, op. cit., p. 303.
13 Quotation from Barrett, *The Rastafarians*, op. cit., p. 77.

14 P. B. Clarke, West Africans at War 1914--1918; 1935--1945 (London: Ethnographica, 1985).
15 Garvey, *Philosophy and Opinions* [2nd edition], 2 vols. [compiled by A. J. Garvey] (London: Frank Cass, 1967), p. 34.
16 P. B. Clarke, *West Africa and Christianity,* op. cit., chap. 6.
17 Ibid.
18 Simpson, *Black Religions in the New World,* op. cit., p. 125.
19 Ibid., p. 127.
20 Ibid., p. 268.
21 Garvey, *Philosophy and Opinions,* op. cit., p. 60.
22 A. J. Garvey, *Garvey and Garveyism* (Kingston: Mona Road, 1963), pp. 11-12.
23 Ibid., p. 20.
24 Ibid., p. 18.
25 Ibid., p. 29.
26 Shepperson, op. cit., p. 307.
27 Ibid.
28 Ibid.
29 Quotation from E. Cashmore, *Rastaman. The Rastafarian Movement in England* [First edition] (London: George Allen and Unwin, 1979), p. 22.

CHAPTER 4

1 Cashmore, *Rastaman,* op. cit., chap. 2, pp. 13 ff.
2 Ibid.
3 Ayodele Taylor's article in *The Daily Service* [Newspaper of the Nigerian Youth Movement] (September 1936).
4 Ibid.
5 Ibid.
6 Clarke, *West Africans at War,* op. cit., chap. 4.
7 Cashmore, *Rastaman,* op. cit., pp. 27-8.
8 Michael Thomas/Adrian Boot, *Jah Revenge* (London: Eel Pie Publishing Ltd., 1982), p. 60.
9 Quotation from L. Kuper, *Race, Class and Power* (London: Duckworth, 1974), p. 179.
10 M. G. Smith, R. Augier and R. Nettleford, *The Rastafari Movement in Kingston, Jamaica* (Kingston: Institute of Social and Economic Research, University of the West Indies, 1960).
11 Cashmore, op. cit., p. 33.
12 W. Rodney, *The Groundings with My Brothers* (London: Bogle-L'Ouverture Publications, 1969).
13 Thomas and Boot, *Jah Revenge* op. cit., p. 70.
14 V. Reckford, 'Rastafarian Music: An Introductory Study', *Jamaica Journal* 11, 1-2 (1977), 11.
15 C. S. Hill, 'Pentecostalist Growth — Result of Racialism?', *Race Today,* Vol. 3, No. 6 (1971), 129-38. See also C. S. Hill and D. Matthews (eds.),

Race — A Christian Symposium (London: Gollancz, 1968).

16 C. S. Hill, *West Indian Migrants and the London Churches* (London: Oxford University Press, 1968).

17 D. G. Nicholls, 'East Indians and Black Power in Trinidad', *Race,* Vol. XII, No. 4 (April 1971), 444.

18 Ibid.

19 Littlewood and Lipsedge, *Aliens and Alienists,* op. cit., p. 44.

20 Ibid.

21 Quotation from Kuper, *Race, Class and Power,* op. cit., p. 84.

22 C. Tullock, 'Revolution and Rhetoric', *Race Today*, Vol. 3, No. 6 (1971) 184--5.

23 Catholic Commission for Racial Justice, Notes and Reports No. 10, *Rastafarians in Jamaica and Britain* (January, 1982). See also Lindsay Mackie, 'Building a Bridge to the Young Rastafarians', *The Guardian* (November 1976).

24 Revd Clifford Mead, Letter to *The Guardian* (October 1981).

25 J. R. Buckholder, 'The Law Knows No Heresy: Marginal Religious Movements and the Courts', in I. Zarestsky and M. Leone (eds.) *Religious Movements in Contemporary America* (Princeton: Princeton University Press, 1974), pp. 27-50.

26 Ibid.

27 Ibid.

28 *The Brixton Disorders 10-12 April 1981: Report of an Inquiry by the Rt. Hon. the Lord Scarman,* OBE (HMSO Cmnd 8427), p. 44, para. 3. 106.

29 Interview material.

30 Interview material.

31 Ibid.

32 Ibid.

33 Ibid.

34 Ibid.

35 Interview.

36 L. A. Goffe, 'Rastas in Ghana, West Africa' (19 November 1984), p. 2320.

37 Interview material.

38 G. S. Peart, 'Rastafarianism — A Christian's Quest into the Understanding of this Cult', *Exodus* (December 1983--January 1984), 9 ff.

39 Information from Professor H. W. Turner, Centre for New Religious Movements, Selly Oak Colleges, Birmingham.

40 Interview material.

CHAPTER 5

1 J. Owens, *Dread. The Rastafarians of Jamaica,* op. cit., p. 3.

2 G. E. Simpson, 'Political Cultism in West Kingston', *Social and Economic Studies,* Vol. 4, No. 2 (1953).

3 Smith, Augier and Nettleford, *The Rastafari Movement in Kingston, Jamaica,* op. cit.

4   W. E. Bowen, 'Rastafarism and The New Society', *Savacou*, No. 5 (June, 1971), 41-50.
5   P. B. Clarke, 'New Paths to Salvation', *Religion Today*, Vol. 1, No. 1 (May, 1984), 1 ff.
6   Owens, *Dread*, op. cit., p. 124.
7   B. R. Wilson, *Magic and the Millennium* (London: Heinemann, 1973).
8   C. Y. Glock and R. Stark, *Religion and Society in Tension* (Chicago: Rand McNally, 1965), pp. 242-59.
9   E. U. Essien-Udom, *Black Nationalism: A Search for Identity in America* (Chicago: University of Chicago Press, 1962).
10 M. Douglas, *Purity and Danger. An Analysis of the Concepts of Pollution and Taboo* (London: Routledge and Kegan Paul, 1978), p. 171.
11 H. W. Turner, *African Independent Church. The Life and Faith of the Church of the Lord (Aladura)* (Oxford: Oxford University Press, 1967), p. 255.
12 One piece of recent evidence for this is the Leeds University study on Conventional Religion in Leeds carried out by members of the departments of Sociology and Theology and Religious Studies at that University. This three-year project was completed in 1983.

CHAPTER 6

1   Interview material.
2   Lynch, *Edward Wilmot Blyden*, op. cit., p. 53.
3   Edward Wilmot Blyden, in H. R. Lynch (ed) *Blyden: Black Spokesman. Selected Published Writings* (London, Frank Cass, 1971), p. 251.
4   Ibid., pp. 250-1.
5   Ibid., p. 253.
6   Ibid., p. 250.
7   Ibid.
8   Interview material.
9   Ibid.
10 Owens, *Dread*, op. cit., p. 276.
11 Interview material.
12 Interview material.
13 See note 11 above.
14 Peart, *Rastafarianism*, op. cit., p. 11.
15 C. Eric Lincoln, *The Black Muslims in America* (Boston: The Beacon's Press, 1961), pp. 48 and 108; E. U. Essien-Udom, *Black Nationalism*, op. cit.
16 Interviews with Rastas.
17 Owens, *Dread*, op. cit., p. 149.
18 Interview material.
19 C. Yawney, 'To Grow a Daughter: Cultural Liberation and the Dynamics of Oppression in Jamaica' in A. Miles and G. Finn (eds.), *Feminism in Canada* (Montreal: Black Rose Press, 1983), p. 121; see also the same authors, *Lions in Babylon: The Rastafarians of Jamaica as a Visionary*

movement, Ph.D. thesis, McGill University (1979).

20 Ibid., 'To Grow a Daughter', p. 123.

21 Ibid., p. 126.

22 Ibid., p. 132.

23 Ibid.

24 Interview material. See also Cashmore, *Rastaman,* op. cit., pp. 78-9.

25 Interview material.

26 This is the case in parts of western Nigeria, where the author carried out field work for a number of years.

27 Owens, *Dread*, op. cit., p. 67.

28 Reckford, *Rastafarian Music,* op. cit; Thomas and Boot, *Jah Revenge,* op. cit.

29 Reckford, *Rastafarian Music,* op. cit., p. 8.

CHAPTER 7

1 Interview material.

2 L. Buñuel, *My Last Breath* (London: Jonathan Cape, 1984), p. 5.

3 A. J. Raboteau, *Slave Religion* (Oxford University Press, 1980), chap. 1 and *passim*.

4 Interviews with non-Rastas, including an Ethiopian.

5 Ibid.

6 *The Brixton Disorders 10-12 April 1981: Report of an Inquiry by the Rt. Hon. The Lord Scarman, OBE* (HMSO Cmnd 8427), p. 44, para 3, 106.

7 Ibid.

8 Interview material.

9 Ibid.

10 Interview material.

11 Interview material.

12 Interview material.

13 E. U. Essien-Udom, *Black Nationalism: A Search for Identity in America.* (University of Chicago Press, Chicago, 1962), p. 14.

Select Bibliography

E. A. Ayandele, *The Missionary Impact on Modern Nigeria 1842-1914. A Political and Social Analysis* (London: Longman, 1966).

L. E. Barret, *The Rastafarians. The Dreadlocks of Jamaica* (Kingston: Sangsters Book Stores Ltd. in association with Heinemann, 1977).

E. W. Blyden, *Christianity, Islam and the Negro Race* (Edinburgh: Edinburgh University Press, 1967).

The Brixton Disorders 10-12 April 1981: Report of an Inquiry by the Rt. Hon. The Lord Scarman, OBE (HMSO Cmnd 8427).

E. Cashmore, *Rastaman. The Rastafarian Movement in England* [first edition] (London: George Allen and Unwin, 1979).

P. B. Clarke, *West Africa and Christianity c. 1450-c.1980* (London: Edward Arnold, 1985).

P. D. Curtin, *The Atlantic Slave Trade: A Census* (Madison: University of Wisconsin Press, 1969).

M. Douglas, *Purity and Danger. An Analysis of the Concepts of Pollution and Taboo* (London: Routledge and Kegan Paul, 1978).

E. U. Essien-Udom, *Black Nationalism: A Search for Identity in America* (Chicago: University of Chicago Press, 1962).

L. Garrison, *Black Youth, Rastafarianism and the Identity Crisis in Britain* (London: An ACER Project Publication, 1979).

A. J. Garvey, *Garvey and Garveyism* (Kingston: Mona Road, 1963).

M. Garvey, *Philosophy and Opinions* (compiled by A. M. Garvey), 2 vols. (London: Frank Cass, 1967).

C. Y. Glock and R. Stark, *Religion and Society in Tension* (Chicago: Rand McNally, 1965).

C. S. Hill, *West Indian Migrants and the London Churches* (London: Oxford University Press, 1968).

C. S. Hill and D. Matthews (eds.), *Race — A Christian Symposium* (London: Gollancz, 1968).

J. E. Inikori (ed.), *Forced Migration. The Impact of the Export Slave Trade on African Societies* (London: Hutchinson University Library, 1981).

R. W. July, *The Origins of Modern African Thought. Its Development in West*

Africa During the Nineteenth and Twentieth Centuries (New York: Prapaer, 1967).

L. Kuper, *Race, Class and Power* (London: Duckworth, 1974).

R. Littlewood and M. Lipsedge, *Alien and Alienists. Ethnic Minorities and Psychiatry* (Harmondsworth, Middlesex: Penguin Books, 1982).

H. R. Lynch, *Edward Wilmot Blyden. Pan-Negro Patriot 1832-1912.* (London: Oxford University Press, 1967).

H. R. Lynch (ed.), *Blyden: Black Spokesman. Selected Published Writings* (London: Frank Cass, 1971).

D. G. Nicholls, 'East Indians and Black Power in Trinidad', *Race,* Vol. XII, No. 4 (April, 1971).

J. Owens, *Dread. The Rastafarians of Jamaica* [with an Introduction by Rex Nettleford] (London: Heinemann, 1979).

J. Peterson, *Province of Freedom* (Evanston, Ill.: Northwestern University Press, 1969).

A. J. Raboteau, *Slave Religion. The 'Invisible Institution' in the Antebellum South* (Oxford: Oxford University Press, 1980).

V. Reckford, 'Rastafarian Music. An Introductory Study *Jamaica Journal* 11 1-2 (1977), 11 ff.

W. Rodney, *The Groundings with My Brothers* (London: Bogle-L'Ouverture Publications, 1969).

T. W. Schick, *Behold The Promised Land* (Baltimore and London: Johns Hopkins University Press, 1977).

G. Shepperson, 'Notes on Negro American Influences On the Emergence of African Nationalism', *Journal of African History,* 1, 2 (1960).

G. E. Simpson, *Black Religions in the New World* (New York: Columbia University Press, 1978).

M. G. Smith, R. Augier and R. Nettleford. *The Rastafari Movement in Kingston, Jamaica* (Institute of Social and Economic Research, University of the West Indies, 1960).

M. Thomas and Adrian Boot, *Jah Revenge* (London: Eel Pie Publishing Ltd., 1982).

K. M. Williams, *The Rastafarians* (London: Ward Lock Educational, 1981).

W. L. Williams, *Black Americans And The Evangelization of Africa 1877-1900* (Madison: University of Wisconsin Press, 1982).

B. R. Wilson, *Magic and the Millennium* (London: Heinemann, 1973).

Index